more
quick-fix
vegan

Other Books by Robin Robertson

Quick-Fix Vegan

Quick-Fix Vegetarian

1,000 Vegan Recipes

Vegan Fire and Spice

Fresh from the Vegan Slow Cooker

Vegan on the Cheap

Nut Butter Universe

One-Dish Vegan

Vegan Planet

Party Vegan

The Vegetarian Meat and Potatoes Cookbook

simple, delicious
recipes in
30 minutes
or less

more
quick-fix
vegan

robin robertson

**Andrews McMeel
Publishing, LLC**
Kansas City • Sydney • London

Andrews McMeel Publishing, LLC
an Andrews McMeel Universal company
1130 Walnut Street, Kansas City, Missouri 64106

14 15 16 17 18 RR2 10 9 8 7 6 5 4 3 2 1

ISBN: 978-1-4494-4613-0

Library of Congress Control Number: 2013914868

Photos courtesy of iStockphoto.com pages v, vi, viii, x, 2, 33, 84, 151, and 170; photos courtesy of Zsu Dever pages 22, 42, 68, 98, 124, 144, 158, and 178

www.andrewsmcmeel.com

www.robinrobertson.com

ATTENTION: SCHOOLS AND BUSINESSES
Andrews McMeel books are available at quantity discounts with bulk purchase for educational, business, or sales promotional use. For information, please e-mail the Andrews McMeel Publishing Special Sales Department: specialsales@amuniversal.com

for the animals and
the people who love them

contents

acknowledgments

I'm eternally grateful to the wonderful people who helped me with this project. First and foremost, I want to express my gratitude to a fantastic group of recipe testers: Barbara Bryan, Jonathan and Nancy Shanes, Lea Jacobson, Lori Maffei, Lyndsay Orwig, Melissa Chapman, and Zsu Dever. Your generous feedback and enthusiasm while testing the recipes for this book are appreciated beyond words.

Many thanks and much love to my husband and best friend, Jon, for being my one-man support system, along with our resident felines: Gary, Mitzki, Jason, Margaret, and Petey.

I also want to thank the talented team at Andrews McMeel Publishing, especially my editor, Jean Lucas, as well as Diane Marsh, Dave Shaw, and Carol Coe. My gratitude also goes to my longtime agent, Stacey Glick, of Dystel & Goderich Literary Management.

introduction

As I write this book, my third volume in the "Quick-Fix" series, one thing is crystal clear: People crave delicious, healthy recipes that don't take long to prepare. I know, because I'm one of them. Food is my life's work, but ironically, I'm often too busy to spend a lot of time cooking. Because healthy, well-balanced meals are important to me, I've devised numerous strategies and techniques to minimize food preparation time, while also maximizing the great flavors and nutrition of what I prepare.

As with my two previous "Quick-Fix" titles, my primary goal in writing *More Quick-Fix Vegan* is to show how easy it is to cook vegan with another 150 recipes that take 30 minutes or less of active preparation time. With these new recipes, using my strategies and techniques, you'll get the same great results as you did in my earlier books for cooking healthy and economical meals even when you're short on time.

This book adds to my collection of easy and delicious recipes using fresh produce, beans, whole grains, pasta, and an arsenal of spices, herbs, and other seasonings. Beginning with a chapter of hearty soups and stews such as Harissa-Spiked Pumpkin Soup (page 32) and Green Chile Stew (page 41), I move onto a huge selection of stir-fries, sautés, and skillet dishes such as Eggplant and Chickpeas Puttanesca (page 71), Fiery Korean Stir-Fry (page 73),

Black Beans and Spinach with Tomato-Avocado Salsa (page 83), and Big Bang Tofu (page 94). Pasta dishes include Jamaican Rasta Pasta (page 106) and Ziti with Creamy Radicchio Sauce (page 112). With these recipes, you'll never be without an answer to the question, "What's for dinner?"

The book also includes a selection of meal-worthy sandwiches such as Tonkatsu Tacos (page 137) and Philly UnCheesesteaks (page 132), a chapter full of "big bowls" recipes, including Romesco Vegetable Bowls (page 46), Balti Bowls (page 54), and Chimichurri Quinoa Bowls (page 56), and several "pantry makes perfect" recipes that use only pantry ingredients for fast and flavorful recipes in a hurry. There is also a chapter titled "From the Oven," which I've filled with recipes that can be put together in less than 30 minutes and then popped into the oven or assembled ahead of time to bake later. The book ends with a dessert chapter filled with sweet endings that are also quick to fix.

I hope you enjoy making the recipes in *More Quick-Fix Vegan* as much as I enjoyed creating them for you.

more
quick-fix
vegan

basically speaking

Before diving into the recipes, I'd like to share with you some basic information, tips, and other ideas to maximize your enjoyment of this book. If you're looking for simple, quick, and delicious recipes that also contain no animal products, then you've come to the right place.

All of the recipes in this book take 30 minutes or less of "active" time to prepare. Because the recipes are easy to make, they are ideally suited for new cooks, new vegans, or for anyone who is short on time but wants to prepare healthy home-cooked meals.

In this chapter, you'll find helpful tips on how to keep a "quick-fix" vegan kitchen, including a pantry list, equipment information, menu-planning and shopping tips, and ways to incorporate convenience foods. I've also included recipes for basic ingredients used throughout the book, including Vegetable Broth (page 13) and Seitan Trio (page 14) for those who want to make them from scratch. A similar chapter of basic information can be found in each of my two earlier volumes, *Quick-Fix Vegetarian* and *Quick-Fix Vegan*, but because this information is so important to "quick-fix" success, I have included many of the basic concepts here too.

more quick-fix vegan basics

The main reason I enjoy developing "quick-fix" vegan recipes is that I want to eliminate any excuse people may have for not going vegan and cooking their own meals. The fact is, vegan cooking is not only quick and easy but it's also flexible and economical. In other words, it's win-win no matter how you look at it.

time-saving strategies

There are a number of strategies to consider in order to minimize the amount of time you spend in the kitchen:

Organize your work space. Before you start cooking, assemble all of the ingredients and equipment you'll need to make a recipe. Measure out the ingredients in advance; this is called *mise en place.* If you do this before you begin to cook, it will save you time, reduce stress, and may even improve your cooking skills by helping you avoid kitchen mishaps, such as realizing you are missing ingredients or burning the onions while you search for a spatula.

Read a recipe all the way through—twice. It's much easier to prepare a recipe when you are familiar with it. Reading through a recipe (especially one that is new to you) will help you avoid any mid-recipe surprises.

Be flexible. Even when we try to plan ahead and have everything we need on hand to make a recipe, sometimes we run out of an ingredient at the last minute. When that happens, don't panic. Just figure out if you have something on hand to substitute for the missing ingredient. To avoid running out of the ingredients you use most frequently, keep a grocery list handy in the kitchen so

you can write down items the minute you run out or are getting low.

Swap it. If you don't like a particular ingredient in a recipe, or perhaps you don't have it on hand, chances are you can still make the recipe. It's often a simple matter of substituting one ingredient for another, such as using white beans instead of chickpeas, or basil instead of cilantro.

Season subjectively. With the help of my dedicated recipe testers, I have done my best to use seasonings in these recipes that should please most palates. However, you should still use your own judgment regarding the use of various herbs and spices, depending on your personal tastes as well as to adjust for variables such as the strength (and saltiness) of your vegetable broth, or the heat of the chiles you may have on hand.

Stock the pantry. The most important component of quick-fix cooking is a well-stocked pantry. The following section will help you get your pantry in order.

a quick-fix pantry

Keep your pantry filled with all the ingredients you use regularly, including canned beans, nuts, dried fruits, and convenience products such as ready-made sauces. When you have a well-stocked pantry, you'll have the satisfaction of knowing that a good meal can always be ready in minutes. Naturally, the wider the variety of ingredients you have, the more choices you will have at dinnertime.

the pantry list

The following is a list of ingredients that you might want to keep on hand to add variety to your menus. With these ingredients, a world of quick and easy meals can be at your fingertips. The list includes basics such as whole grains, pasta, and beans, as well as several condiments, sauces, and other ingredients. Use this list as a guideline to develop your own pantry list according to your personal taste.

BASICS

- **Beans:** Keep a variety of dried beans on hand. To use them in quick-fix meals, you can cook dried beans in large batches and then portion and freeze them for ease of use. I also suggest keeping a supply of canned beans on hand, such as black beans, chickpeas, kidney beans, pintos, and cannellini beans. A can of beans can be a lifesaver on busy weeknights. Protein-rich beans are a great addition to pasta and grain dishes, as well as vegetable dishes and salads. Beans can be pureed for sauces, dips, and spreads or mashed to make loaves, burgers, and more.

- **Grains:** Remember that certain grains cook faster than others, so every quick-fix kitchen should have quinoa and bulgur on hand, as well as couscous and quick-cooking brown rice. For convenience, any longer-cooking grains, such as brown rice, can be prepared in large batches, portioned, and stored in the freezer.

- **Pasta and noodles:** Keep a variety of pasta shapes on hand, including quick-cooking capellini, as well as orzo, thin rice noodles, and buckwheat soba.

- **Gnocchi and polenta:** Shelf-stable vegan gnocchi cook up in 3 minutes and can be used as a change of pace from pasta, potatoes, or grains. Polenta is available refrigerated in a log shape or in a shelf-stable rectangular shape and is great topped with chili or marinara sauce.

- **Flour tortillas, lavash, and other flat-breads:** In addition to making burritos, fajitas, and quesadillas, you can use tortillas and other flatbreads to make wrap sandwiches, layered casseroles, and even super-thin-crust pizzas.

- **Pizza dough:** Buy ready-to-bake pizza dough to make quick and easy pizzas with your favorite toppings, or keep a stash of homemade Pizza Dough (page 16) in the freezer.

- **Piecrust or dough:** Frozen ready-to-use vegan piecrusts can come in handy. More economical is your own homemade Pie Dough (page 18), individually wrapped and frozen. When ready to use, just thaw and roll out. Frozen vegan puff pastry, such as the Pepperidge Farm brand that is available in most supermarkets, is also handy to keep in the freezer.

- **Vegetable broth:** A world of choices awaits, from homemade broth portioned and frozen to prepared broths in cans or aseptic containers. There is also a variety of vegetable broth pastes, powders, and cubes that are as convenient as they come—just add water (see page 7)!

- **Nondairy milk:** There is a wide variety of nondairy milks available, including soy, rice, and almond milks. You can buy them in refrigerated cartons or aseptic packages. Many varieties come in different flavors, including unsweetened as well as plain, vanilla, and chocolate.

- **Unsweetened coconut milk:** Used in many Asian dishes, unsweetened coconut milk can also be used to enrich desserts, sauces, and other recipes.

- **Tomato products:** Canned tomatoes are practical and versatile and come in many forms, including diced, whole, puree, and paste.

- **Bottled marinara sauce:** Nothing beats the flavor of homemade marinara sauce, but keeping a jar of prepared sauce on hand can help you get a pasta meal on the table in minutes. Add a splash of red wine, fresh herbs, or sautéed mushrooms to give the sauce a homemade touch.

BEYOND THE BASICS

In addition to the previous ingredients, there are several others that I like to keep on hand. I refer to these beyond-the-basics ingredients as "flavor makers." This list is by no means comprehensive, so use it as a guide and add any favorite sauces, seasonings, or other ingredients that can help "make" the meal.

- artichoke hearts (canned and frozen)
- barbecue sauce
- capers
- dried chiles
- roasted red peppers
- chipotle chiles in adobo
- hot chili paste
- chutney
- curry paste or powder
- dried fruits: raisins, cranberries, apricots, and so on
- minced ginger (in a jar or tube)
- hoisin sauce
- miso paste
- nutritional yeast
- nut butters: peanut, almond, and so on
- nuts and seeds
- olive tapenade
- olives (black and green)
- tamari soy sauce
- sriracha sauce

- sun-dried tomatoes (dried and packed in oil)
- tahini (sesame paste)
- tomato salsa

ingredient shortcuts

Another key element to quick-fix success is to plan ahead regarding certain ingredients that may need advance preparation, as in the case of dried beans. For example, in order to be ready in 30 minutes, recipes using beans will call for cooked or canned beans. It is up to you whether you choose to cook your beans from the dried state (see page 5) and portion and freeze them, or whether you prefer to buy canned beans to keep in your pantry. (I do both.)

You will find that certain recipes in this book call for other ingredients that can either be made in advance from scratch or purchased at the store. If you opt for store-bought, then all you need to do is stock your pantry. If you prefer to go the homemade route, then you need to keep a supply of those foods prepared and on hand.

Whether planning ahead means keeping containers of vegetable stock and beans in the freezer or buying canned vegetable broth and beans for the cupboard, the important thing is to keep essential ingredients on hand to prevent time-wasting extra shopping trips for one or two ingredients.

Without question, cooking beans and grains from scratch and making homemade broth are the best choices both nutritionally and economically. However, with today's hectic pace, cooking with canned beans and quick-cooking rice may be the only way some people can manage to cook healthy vegan meals. If you prefer to make certain ingredients from scratch, you'll save time if you plan ahead and portion and freeze ingredients such as beans and longer-cooking grains as described here.

Since a 15- to 16-ounce can of beans contains about 1½ cups of beans, it's a good idea to portion and freeze your home-cooked beans in the same amounts. On average, 1 pound of dried beans will yield 4 to 6 cups cooked (depending on the bean), or the equivalent of three to four cans.

Other prepared-ingredient shortcuts that can help save time are jarred roasted red bell peppers and bottled minced ginger. I also like to keep a bag of frozen bell pepper strips on hand for times when I only need a small amount of bell pepper for a recipe, when I've run out of fresh ones, or when the fresh bell peppers are too expensive.

Peeled garlic cloves, available in a jar in the produce section of the supermarket, are convenient time-savers. While minced garlic is also available in jars, I prefer the flavor quality of the whole peeled garlic cloves. A jar of peeled garlic cloves can also be a handy backup when what remains of your fresh garlic bulb has sprouted or dried up.

about vegetable broth

If you prefer not to make homemade broth (see page 13), prepared vegetable broth is available in cans and aseptic containers at well-stocked supermarkets and natural food stores. The strength and flavor of the broth varies greatly by brand, so try a couple and decide which one you like best. Other choices include vegan bouillon cubes, powdered vegetable base, and vegetable broth paste. These products are easy and economical to use, and they can be made into broth with the addition of boiling water.

Be aware that the saltiness of the different broths can vary widely (including homemade). As broth reduces while cooking, the saltiness increases, so you'll need to judge the saltiness as you cook. For these reasons, many of the recipes in this book call for salt to be added "to taste."

As with any packaged food, check the ingredients for additives and buy the healthiest one (often the one with the least number of ingredients as well as those lower in sodium).

When using broths, initially taste them for strength, since some have stronger flavors that may encroach on the flavor of your finished dish. For a milder broth that is also more economical, dilute the canned broth by adding the equivalent amount of water. For example, if a recipe calls for 4 cups of broth, you can use one can of broth (approximately 2 cups) plus 2 cups of water.

vegetable choices

Whenever possible, it's best to use fresh, organic, locally grown produce. However, it's important to be realistic and realize that sometimes fresh organic produce is not available in the varieties we need, is too expensive for the household budget, or is out of season. Also, if you limit your shopping to once per week, you may not be able to buy enough fresh produce to last until your next shopping trip.

One solution can be to incorporate some frozen vegetables into your meals later in the week. Frozen veggies are already prepped and easy to use. Since they are frozen when they are freshly picked, they can be fresher than the "fresh" veggies in your supermarket, which may have been picked early and shipped long distances. Frozen veggies are also economical, they cook quickly, and they can help you get through the week with quick and healthy meals.

Some frozen vegetables that find their way into my cooking include artichoke hearts, baby green peas, bell pepper strips, chopped spinach, corn kernels, and edamame. When fresh veggies aren't available, I also use some canned vegetables, especially tomatoes and tomato products, artichoke hearts, solid-pack pumpkin, and, of course, canned beans of all kinds.

Even within the realm of fresh vegetables, there are convenience items that you can use to minimize prep time, including a wide variety of prewashed and prepared salad mixes, from baby spinach to mixed field greens to crunchy romaine. If you use a bottled dressing (or have homemade dressing on hand), your salad will be ready in seconds.

Also convenient are baby carrots, because they can be used without having to be peeled. Like bagged lettuces, bagged shredded cabbage is available, primarily for coleslaw, but it's also ideal when recipes call for shredded cabbage. For those in an unrelenting time crunch, you can save even more time by using pre-sliced mushrooms, pre-chopped fresh onions, and bags of fresh stir-fry vegetables.

Whenever you use pre-cut vegetables, however, even those that are labeled "washed and ready to use," I recommend washing them again, just to be safe.

nondairy milk and other nondairy ingredients

Nondairy milks, including those made from soy, almonds, rice, and oats, can be used in recipes in the same way dairy milk is used. For savory recipes, it's important to use unsweetened varieties, however, since some brands of nondairy milk contain added sugar, even those labeled "plain." My personal favorite nondairy milk is almond milk—I use the plain unsweetened variety in both savory and sweet recipes in this book, but if

you prefer to use another type of nondairy milk, feel free to do so.

Other products, such as vegan versions of mayonnaise, cream cheese, sour cream, yogurt, and various types of cheese, are available to use instead of dairy products.

tofu, tempeh, and seitan

Protein-rich foods such as tempeh, tofu, and seitan are popular plant-based alternatives to meat. In addition to these mainstays, prepared vegan protein options include veggie burgers, sausages, and burger crumbles. These products can be used to replace meat in recipes that normally call for meat, or they can be enjoyed in interesting new ways.

While tofu and tempeh are widely available and reasonably priced, prepared seitan can be expensive and may be harder to find in some regions. In addition, depending on how it is packaged, each brand of seitan can have different flavors from its marinating liquid that might interfere with your recipe. On the other hand, homemade seitan is simple and economical to make. On page 14 you will find a basic seitan recipe that can be made three different ways: on top of the stove, in the oven, or in a slow cooker. You can also vary the seasonings according to taste. Once cooled, seitan can be wrapped and refrigerated or frozen to use in recipes. Properly stored, seitan will keep well in the refrigerator for 3 to 4 days and in the freezer for 3 months.

other ingredients

In an effort to make this book user-friendly, I've done my best to use easy-to-find ingredients in the recipes. I don't want you to avoid a recipe simply because you can't find a particular ingredient. At the same time, if you have personal preferences, feel free to substitute ingredients you like for ones that you don't. For example, if you don't enjoy the kidney beans called for in a recipe, but you love chickpeas, go ahead and use the chickpeas instead. As mentioned earlier, this applies to seasonings as well. If you prefer more or less of certain seasonings, feel free to season foods according to your own taste.

You may notice that some recipes call for hard vegetables such as carrots to be thinly sliced, finely chopped, or shredded. This is because the thinner a vegetable is sliced, the quicker it will cook.

When olive oil is listed in a recipe, it refers to extra-virgin olive oil. When salt is listed, sea salt is preferred. When chopped scallions (aka green onions) are listed, it refers to both the white and green parts. For sugar, I recommend an organic natural sugar such as Sucanat.

When specific can or jar sizes are called for, these sizes are based on what is available in my local store. If your store carries 15-ounce cans of beans and the recipe calls for a 16-ounce can, go with the size found in your store. Such a small size differentiation won't affect the recipe results.

plan ahead

Some advance planning in the form of an ongoing grocery list and menu plan for the week are the best ways to ensure that you can get dinner on the table in 30 minutes or less. Here are some ways to incorporate list making into your routine:

Keep a list of your family's favorite dishes and rotate them regularly.

Plan meals in advance, serving make-ahead one-dish meals on especially busy nights.

Plan your menus. This doesn't have to be a complete formal menu plan. Instead, just make a brief note such as: "Monday: tacos; Tuesday: tofu stir-fry; Wednesday: pasta and salad"; and so on. Having an idea of your menu for the week will help you with your grocery shopping and save you time all week long. Refer to this list when you make your grocery list so you'll have all your ingredients on hand when you need them.

Make a master grocery list once and photocopy it for future use.

Keep your grocery list handy to jot items on the list as they become low.

Organize your pantry shelves so you know where everything is at a glance.

Keep a variety of condiments on hand that add flavor to a recipe, such as soy sauce, sriracha or other hot sauce, chutney, and salsa.

Save time at the supermarket by being familiar with the store layout (many grocery stores have maps of their layout) and write your grocery list in the same order that you will be walking through the store aisles.

Take advantage of sales and have some flexibility regarding ingredient choices. For example, when the store has a sale on asparagus, you may want to buy extra to enjoy before the price goes back up.

quick-fix cook-a-thons

When time is at a premium, consider doing a weekly cook-a-thon during which you prepare several meals at once. Set aside a few hours to spend in the kitchen—I usually schedule mine on Sunday afternoons, when I put on some music and prepare a few dishes to get me through the week. I like to prepare things that reheat well or that can be portioned and frozen, such as a pot of chili, a hearty soup, a casserole, or a grain pilaf. It's also a great time to cook a big batch of brown rice, dried beans, or vegetable broth to portion and freeze.

Here are some guidelines for cook-a-thons:

- Prepare double batches of long-cooking recipes, such as stews, soups, or chili. Bonus: Their flavor improves when reheated, so they're even better when served later in the week or after being frozen for a time.

- Cook a large pot of a staple grain or bean—I usually make a different kind of bean each week, so that I can have a variety portioned and frozen for later use. When you need them, just thaw and heat.

- Double up on prep work, such as chopping onions, when making more than one recipe, so you have enough for both. When you only need half an onion, chop the whole onion and refrigerate the unused portion in a sealed bag.

- Wash and dry lettuces and other vegetables when you bring them home from the store. This will save you time when you want to make a quick meal.

love those leftovers

I love leftovers. Not just those soups or stews that taste even better reheated—I even enjoy the solitary leftover baked potato or that small amount of vegetables that was overlooked last night at dinner. Leftovers are fun to transform into an entirely different second meal. This not only helps if you have family members who don't like to eat the same thing two days in a row but it's also economical, since it can help stretch your food dollar and eliminate waste. With a little ingenuity, there are lots of creative ways to use leftovers. For example, that leftover potato can be diced or sliced and sautéed with chopped onions, oregano, and lemon juice for a terrific side dish of Greek-style potatoes. You could also mash it up with some leftover vegetables and make fritters, a tofu scramble, or even a stuffing for samosas.

I often make dinner with a second meal in mind. Chili is a prime example. You can enjoy the chili "as is" one day and then use the leftovers to make a layered Mexican-style casserole with soft tortillas, salsa, and other ingredients. Spoon leftover stew into a casserole dish, top with a ready-to-use piecrust, and pop it into the oven for a quick and easy pot pie. Puree a small amount of leftover vegetable soup to use in a flavorful primavera sauce for pasta. Just as leftover vegetables can be used in a quiche or casserole or added to composed salads or pasta and grain dishes, so too can a small amount of leftover pasta, potatoes, or rice be added to salads or soups for a hearty main-dish meal.

Begin to think about preparing food that can be incorporated into another meal. For example, if you only need half of a box of pasta for a meal, cook the entire box anyway. Having extra cooked pasta on hand can save time when making dinner another night, by using the pasta in a different way.

homemade convenience foods

"Ready-made" at the supermarket will save time when preparing a meal. The downside to that convenience is the added expense. You can make many such convenience foods, such as broth and pizza dough, at home in quantity, and then portion and freeze them. One of the most economical items to make from scratch is vegetable broth. A recipe for homemade broth, as well as other homemade convenience foods including seitan, pie dough, and pizza dough, can be found in this chapter, beginning on page 13.

kitchen equipment

While good kitchen equipment is important, I believe that cooking is more about the person doing the cooking and the quality of the ingredients. Buy the best-quality equipment you can afford, but you don't necessarily need to have a huge set of pots and pans (or other equipment) when just a few will do.

Every kitchen needs at least one pot big enough to boil pasta and make several quarts of vegetable broth. You also need a couple of smaller saucepans, including one with a steamer insert for steaming vegetables. Two or three heavy-bottomed skillets, ranging in size from 8 to 18 inches in diameter, are a must. At least one skillet should have a nonstick surface. All pots and skillets should have lids that fit well.

Other kitchen basics include a few mixing bowls, a set of measuring cups and spoons, a colander, cutting boards, and baking dishes and pans. Nothing much beyond these is required to make the recipes in this book.

In addition, there are a few kitchen tools that can help make cooking faster and easier. They include:

- **Knives.** There are three knives that no kitchen should be without: a paring knife for peeling and trimming; a long serrated knife for slicing bread, tomatoes, and other fragile foods; and a good (8- or 10-inch) chef's knife for virtually everything else. Buy the best-quality knives you can afford and keep them sharp. You can chop more quickly and safely with sharp knives than dull ones.

- **Food processor.** A food processor is essential for making pesto, pureeing vegetables, chopping nuts, and making bread crumbs. It is also great for making pie dough, chopping vegetables, and numerous other mixing and chopping tasks. The trick is knowing when it will be faster to cut, whisk, or chop by hand, and that can usually be determined by the quantity of food involved. In addition to a large-capacity processor, some people also have a smaller model that they use for smaller tasks.

- **Blender.** For the longest time, I got along with just a food processor and no blender at all. Then I acquired a high-powered blender (a Vitamix) and my cooking habits changed. I now use both blender and food processor for different purposes. The blender is reserved for smoothies, sauces, soups, and anything I want to make supersmooth and creamy very quickly. Another plus of having both a food processor and a blender in play is that, when making multiple recipes, I can often avoid stopping to wash out one or the other.

- **Immersion blender.** The advantage to the immersion blender is that it is easier to clean than a regular blender, and it saves the time of pouring your recipe into a blender container, since you can blend the food right in the bowl. It's especially handy for pureeing soup right in the pot.

- **Box grater.** This versatile tool is great when you have a small amount of food that needs grating or shredding (instead of dirtying the food processor). It works well for anything from citrus zest to cabbage. For extra-small jobs, use a Microplane grater.

- **Mandoline.** I use a mandoline when I need very thin slices very fast. Sure, you can always slice ingredients with a knife or even the slicing attachment of a food processor, but this handy gadget lets you cut uniform slices, from thick to paper-thin, with ease and swiftness—just watch your fingers because the blades are extremely sharp. note: The plastic Benriner slicer is a smaller version of the stainless-steel mandoline and is much less expensive, making it a good choice if you're on a budget.

- **Salad spinner.** This is the easiest and quickest way to dry your salad greens after washing them gets every drop of water off your lettuce, leaving it crisp and ready for your salad.

- **Vegetable peeler.** It's quick, easy, and very low-tech, and indispensable for peeling carrots, potatoes, cucumbers, and more.

- **Microwave.** While I'd never actually cook dinner in a microwave, it can be a useful tool to help get dinner on the table. It's ideal when you need a small amount of melted vegan butter, chocolate, or hot liquid. You can also use it to soften hard winter squashes to make them easier to cut.

convenience foods from scratch

One of the key points to getting dinner on the table in 30 minutes or less is having all the necessary ingredients handy. Some ingredients are naturally quick cooking, while others need to be made ahead or purchased ready-made at the store. One obvious example is pizza. In order to prepare a pizza in less than 30 minutes, you'll need to have the dough ready in advance. You can either make the dough from scratch ahead of time or you can buy ready-made dough and store it in the refrigerator or freezer. Even though I like to make my own dough, I like to keep a couple of store-bought dough balls in the freezer for emergencies—and I'm always glad I have them!

A few of these basic "convenience" foods are easy and economical to make from scratch. It's up to you to decide if you can take the time to prepare these ingredients ahead so that they're available when you need them or if you prefer the convenience of buying them ready-made, even though it will cost you more. The following are the recipes and cooking instructions for some of the items frequently called for in this book. I've also included descriptions of the store-bought versions of these ingredients, which can be found at well-stocked supermarkets and natural food stores.

In addition, you will find instructions on how to toast nuts and roast bell peppers, both of which can also be bought prepared but are easy to make at home.

basic recipes

vegetable broth

makes about 2 quarts

You can cool and freeze this basic vegetable broth in several storage containers with tight-fitting lids so that you can defrost exactly what you need for a recipe. Be sure to scrub and wash all vegetables well before using. For information on commercial vegetable broths, vegan bouillon cubes, and powdered vegetable base, see page 7.

1 tablespoon olive oil
1 large yellow onion, coarsely chopped
2 large carrots, coarsely chopped
1 large russet potato, cut into chunks
2 celery ribs, including leaves, coarsely chopped
3 cloves garlic, crushed

3 quarts water
2 tablespoons soy sauce
1 cup coarsely chopped fresh Italian parsley
2 bay leaves
½ teaspoon salt
½ teaspoon black peppercorns

Heat the oil in a large stockpot over medium heat. Add the onion, carrots, potato, celery, and garlic. Cover and cook until slightly softened, about 5 minutes. Add the water, soy sauce, parsley, bay leaves, salt, and peppercorns. Bring to a boil, then lower the heat to medium-low and simmer, uncovered, for 1 hour to reduce the liquid by about one-third and bring out the flavors of the vegetables.

Strain the liquid through a fine-mesh sieve into another pot, pressing the juices out of the vegetables with the back of a large spoon. The broth is now ready to use. For a stronger broth, bring the broth back to a boil, and reduce the volume by one-quarter. This broth keeps well in the refrigerator for up to 3 days if kept tightly covered, or you can portion and freeze it for up to 4 months.

seitan trio

makes about 2 pounds

This is my go-to seitan recipe, which you can make on the stovetop, in the oven, or in a slow cooker. It makes about 2 pounds that can be divided into 8-ounce portions, tightly wrapped, and frozen for later use. You can also keep seitan in the refrigerator for up to 3 days, either in a covered container in its cooking broth or portioned and tightly wrapped. This seitan can be used in any of the recipes in this book that call for seitan.

2 cups vital wheat gluten flour
¼ cup nutritional yeast
3 tablespoons tapioca flour
1 teaspoon garlic powder
1 teaspoon onion powder
½ teaspoon salt

¼ teaspoon freshly ground black pepper
1½ cups cold water
2 tablespoons tamari soy sauce
2 tablespoons olive oil
4 cups vegetable broth (for stovetop
   and slow cooker methods)

In a food processor or bowl, combine the vital wheat gluten flour, nutritional yeast, tapioca flour, garlic powder, onion powder, salt, and pepper and pulse or stir to mix. Add the water, tamari, and oil and process or stir to mix well. Turn the mixture out onto a flat surface and knead for 2 minutes or until the dough comes together. Let the dough rest for 5 minutes.

Stovetop: Divide the dough into 4 equal pieces and place them in a large pot with enough cold vegetable broth to cover. Bring almost to a boil, then lower the heat to a simmer and cook for 1 hour. Let the seitan cool in the broth, then refrigerate until firm. The seitan can now be cut or sliced to use in recipes. It will keep refrigerated for up to 3 days or tightly wrapped and frozen for up to 3 months.

Slow Cooker: Divide the dough into 4 equal pieces and place them in a slow cooker with enough vegetable broth to cover. Cook on Low for 8 hours. Cool to room temperature in the slow cooker, then refrigerate until firm. The seitan can now be cut or sliced to use in recipes. It will keep refrigerated for up to 3 days or tightly wrapped and frozen for up to 3 months.

Oven: Preheat the oven to 350°F. Flatten the seitan into a 6-inch square and enclose it loosely in a sheet of aluminum foil. Place the seitan packet in a shallow baking dish and add enough water to come halfway up the seitan packet. Cover the baking pan tightly with foil and bake for 1 hour. Remove the seitan from the pan, remove the foil, and set aside to cool, then refrigerate until firm. The seitan can now be cut or sliced to use in recipes. It will keep refrigerated for up to 3 days or tightly wrapped and frozen for up to 3 months.

baked marinated tofu

serves 4

Packages of prepared baked tofu are available in well-stocked supermarkets and natural food stores in a variety of flavors. They are delicious and easy to use, but they can also be expensive. With this recipe, you can make it yourself at home.

1 cup water
¼ cup soy sauce
2 tablespoons nutritional yeast

½ teaspoon onion powder
1 pound extra-firm tofu, drained

In a shallow bowl or baking dish, combine the water, soy sauce, nutritional yeast, and onion powder. Mix well.

Cut the tofu into ½-inch slices and place in the marinade so that the tofu is covered with the marinade. Cover and refrigerate for several hours or overnight, turning the tofu occasionally if it isn't all submerged in the liquid.

Preheat the oven to 400°F. Lightly oil a large baking sheet. Arrange the marinated tofu slices in a single layer on the baking sheet. Bake for about 30 minutes, turning once about halfway through. If not using right away, cool to room temperature, then store in a tightly covered container in the refrigerator for up to 4 days.

pizza dough

makes enough for 2 (12-inch) pizzas

I always make enough dough for two pizzas at a time (even when I only need one). That way I can stash the extra dough in the freezer for a future meal. I find it quicker to make the dough in a food processor, but you can make it in a stand mixer or in a bowl by hand, if you prefer. For extra flavor, add 1 teaspoon garlic powder or 1 teaspoon dried Italian seasoning to the dough. If not using right away, the dough can be tightly wrapped and frozen for 2 to 3 months, then thawed in the refrigerator and brought to room temperature before shaping into a crust and baking. You can use this dough to make the pizza recipes on pages 169 and 171, or invent your own, adding the toppings of your choice and baking at 450°F for about 10 minutes.

3 cups unbleached all-purpose flour
2¼ teaspoons instant-rise yeast
1¼ teaspoons salt

½ teaspoon natural sugar
1½ tablespoons olive oil
1 cup warm water

Lightly oil the inside of a large bowl with olive oil and set aside. In a food processor (or using a stand mixer fitted with the dough hook), combine the flour, yeast, salt, and sugar. With the machine running, add the oil through the feed tube and then slowly add the water as needed until it forms a slightly sticky dough ball.

Transfer the dough to a floured surface and knead until it is smooth and elastic, 1 to 2 minutes. Use your hands to shape the dough into a smooth ball and place it in the prepared bowl. Turn the dough to coat it with oil, then cover the bowl with plastic wrap and let the dough rise at room temperature in a warm area until doubled in size, about 1 hour.

Punch down the dough and divide it into 2 pieces. On a lightly floured surface, shape each piece into a ball. Cover and let it rest for about 30 minutes. The dough is now ready to use.

beans from scratch

makes about 6 cups

There are several ways to cook beans from scratch. Some people use a pressure cooker, others prefer the stovetop method. I prefer to cook beans in the slow cooker because I can literally "set it and forget it," making this method the least hands-on way to cook beans. Therefore, even though the cooking time is longer, it's less time you need to be in the kitchen. I usually use a 5- to 6-quart slow cooker so that I can cook a large batch at a time, but if you have a smaller cooker, then you can just cook a smaller batch. Dried beans expand when soaked and cooked. Most beans are done cooking in a slow cooker after 8 to 10 hours on Low (or about 4 hours on High), although some may take longer, depending on the age and variety of bean, while others are done much sooner. Except for lentils and split peas, beans should be soaked before cooking to shorten the cooking time and make them more digestible.

1 pound dried beans (any variety),
   picked over and rinsed
2 tablespoons salt

1 large yellow onion, quartered (optional)
2 bay leaves (optional)

Bring 2 quarts of water to a boil in a large pot. Remove from the heat and add the beans and salt, stirring to dissolve the salt. Set aside at room temperature to soak for 1 hour, then drain the beans, discard the soaking liquid, and rinse the beans.

Place the drained, soaked beans in a large slow cooker. Add the onion and bay leaves, if using, and enough water to cover, 6 to 8 cups. Cover and cook on Low for 8 to 12 hours, more or less, depending on the type of bean.

pie dough

makes enough for 2 (9-inch) crusts

This recipe makes enough for one double-crust pie or two single-crust pies. Even if you only need one crust, it's a good idea to make the whole recipe, then freeze the extra dough for when you need it. Then simply thaw and roll out. Frozen piecrusts (in aluminum pie plates) are available in supermarkets and natural food stores. Be sure to read the labels carefully, since some brands may contain lard or butter.

2 cups unbleached all-purpose flour
1 teaspoon salt
⅔ cup vegan butter, cut into small pieces

4 tablespoons ice water,
    or more if needed

Combine the flour and salt in a food processor. Blend in the vegan butter with short pulses until the mixture becomes crumbly. With the machine running, add the water through the feed tube and blend until the dough just starts to hold together. Transfer the dough to a work surface, divide it in half, and flatten to form 2 disks, each about 5 inches in diameter. Wrap the dough in plastic wrap and refrigerate for 30 minutes.

vegan sour cream

makes 1½ cups

12 ounces extra-firm silken tofu, drained
1½ tablespoons rice vinegar
1½ tablespoons freshly
    squeezed lemon juice

2 teaspoons tahini
½ teaspoon salt
½ teaspoon natural sugar

Combine all of the ingredients in a high-speed blender or food processor and process until very smooth. Taste and adjust the seasonings, if needed. Transfer to a tightly covered container and store in the refrigerator for up to 5 days.

vegan mayonnaise

makes about 1½ cups

You can buy vegan mayonnaise (and sour cream and cream cheese) in well-stocked supermarkets and natural food stores. It's also easy to make at home using this recipe.

12 ounces extra-firm silken tofu, drained
2 tablespoons olive oil or grapeseed oil
2 tablespoons cider vinegar

1 teaspoon salt
¼ teaspoon dry mustard

Combine all of the ingredients in a high-speed blender or food processor and process until very smooth. Taste and adjust the seasonings, if needed. Transfer to a tightly covered container and store in the refrigerator for up to 5 days.

vegan cream cheese

makes 1½ cups

½ cup raw cashews, soaked in
   water for 3 hours or overnight
1 cup extra-firm silken tofu

2 tablespoons freshly
   squeezed lemon juice
⅛ teaspoon salt

Drain the cashews, then transfer them to a food processor or high-speed blender. Process until ground to a paste. Loosen the cashews from the bottom of the food processor or blender, then add the tofu, lemon juice, and salt. Process for several minutes, until very smooth, scraping the mixture from the sides of the machine as needed.

If not using immediately, transfer to a tightly covered container and store in the refrigerator for up to 5 days.

roasted bell peppers

You can find 6-ounce and 12-ounce jars of roasted red bell peppers in supermarkets. In terms of convenience, jarred roasted bell peppers can't be beat. However, if you prefer to roast fresh bell peppers, you will be rewarded with richly flavored peppers that outshine those in a jar. I keep a jar or two of roasted peppers on hand, but whenever I have the time or want to make a dish extra-special, I take the time to roast fresh peppers.

Stovetop: You can roast bell peppers directly over the gas flame on your stovetop by holding the pepper over the flame with tongs and turning frequently to allow the skin to blister and blacken.

Grill: You can also roast whole peppers on a grill, turning frequently until charred.

Oven: To roast peppers in the oven, place the peppers directly on the oven rack and roast or broil until blistered and charred.

No matter how you roast them, when the peppers are charred, close them inside a paper or plastic bag. Let cool for 10 minutes, then remove the peppers from the bag and remove the skin. Cut out the stem and slice the peppers open. Remove the core and seeds and cut into pieces. Store in a tightly sealed container in the refrigerator for up to 5 days.

toasted nuts and seeds

Toasting nuts and seeds is easy, and it can deepen their flavor. You can toast them either in a dry skillet on top of the stove or on a baking pan in the oven.

Stovetop: To toast nuts or seeds on the stovetop, place them in a small dry skillet over medium heat and toast them, stirring or shaking the pan occasionally, until lightly browned, 1 to 5 minutes depending on the nut. Be careful not to burn them. Let cool completely.

Oven: To toast nuts or seeds in the oven, preheat the oven to 350°F. Place the nuts in a single layer in a small shallow baking pan. Toast until very lightly browned and fragrant, stirring occasionally, 2 to 8 minutes depending on the type of nut. Pine nuts, sliced almonds, and sesame seeds, for example, begin to brown very quickly, while heartier nuts such as walnuts and pecans take longer. Remove the toasted nuts from the oven and let cool completely.

about the recipes

One thing you may notice about this third volume in the "Quick-Fix" series is that there are more main dishes. This is in response to the many requests I've received for more quick and easy dinner ideas. In addition to a chapter filled with stir-fries, sautés, and skillet dishes, there are chapters devoted to pasta recipes, make-ahead oven recipes, hearty sandwiches that "make a meal," and substantial soups and stews.

I've also included a chapter titled "Big Bowls" filled with recipes combining various components harmoniously to be enjoyed in—you guessed it—a big bowl. You'll also discover a chapter called "Pantry Makes Perfect," which consists of several fun recipes that rely only on pantry ingredients for those times when there's nothing in the fridge and no time to shop. The final chapter is devoted to quick-fix desserts, because—let's face it—even the busiest people need something sweet once in a while.

what do i mean by "active time"?

As with my other quick-fix books, the recipes in this volume take no longer than 30 minutes of active time to prepare. By "active time," I mean the actual hands-on time it takes to prepare the recipe. It does not include the time it takes to gather your equipment and ingredients together or wash your produce. It also doesn't include the time to make your own seitan, pie dough, pizza dough, or other basic ingredient that can be purchased ready-made or should be made in advance.

from the oven

The recipes in "From the Oven" also adhere to less than 30 minutes of "active time," but that doesn't include the in-oven baking time. Those oven-baked recipes are especially convenient because they can be assembled ahead of time and then baked right before you're ready to serve them. Plus, since you bake and serve right in the same baking dish, there's no messy cleanup to worry about. In terms of convenience and variety, recipes that can be assembled ahead of time can actually be the quickest-to-fix meals of all.

oil-free option

You may also notice that most of the recipes in this book offer you the option of using no added oil. This is especially true in the case of sautéed ingredients, where you will see a choice of sautéing in a small amount of oil or water, as you may prefer.

chapter 2

souper soups and stews

When is a soup more than a soup? The answer is: when it's hearty enough to also be lunch or dinner. That's what you'll find in this chapter—soups that are so satisfying that they can be enjoyed as meals, alone or perhaps with the addition of toasted bread and a salad.

Although we often think of soup as something that simmers for hours on the stove, you'll discover that the recipes in this chapter shatter that stereotype. However, like most soups, they do taste even better when reheated the following day.

Within 30 minutes, you can be enjoying a bowl of Smoky Corn Chowder (page 35), French White Bean Soup (page 31), or spicy Harissa-Spiked Pumpkin Soup (page 32). Other flavorful choices include Black Bean–Pumpkin Soup (page 34), fragrant Thai Coconut Soup with Tofu (page 39), and creamy Hummus Soup with Pita Croutons (page 27).

When it comes to vegetable broth, it's up to you whether you use homemade broth (page 13), a commercially prepared broth, or a broth made with water and your favorite brand of vegetable base. Because the amount of salt will vary from broth to broth, it's important that you add salt to these recipes according to your own taste.

shortcut bean soup

serves 4

When you combine canned beans (or thawed frozen beans from your own stash) and just the right amount of seasonings, and then puree some of it, the result tastes like one of those long-cooking bean soups that took all day to simmer. I especially like this combination of black, kidney, and pinto beans for their varying color, texture, and flavors, but you can use any combination you prefer (or even just a single type).

1 tablespoon olive oil or ¼ cup water
1 large yellow onion, chopped
1 carrot, chopped
3 cloves garlic, minced
1 teaspoon ground cumin
1 teaspoon smoked paprika
½ teaspoon dried oregano
1 (14.5-ounce) can diced fire-roasted
    tomatoes, including juices
2 cups vegetable broth
1½ cups home-cooked black beans, or
    1 (15.5-ounce) can, drained and rinsed

1½ cups home-cooked dark red
    kidney beans, or 1 (15.5-ounce)
    can, drained and rinsed
3 cups home-cooked pinto beans, or
    2 (15.5-ounce) cans, drained and rinsed
1 (4-ounce) can chopped mild
    green chiles, drained
Salt and freshly ground black pepper
1 teaspoon hot sauce
½ to 1 teaspoon liquid smoke

Heat the oil in a large pot over medium heat. Add the onion, carrot, and garlic. Cover and cook for 5 minutes to soften. Stir in the cumin, paprika, oregano, tomatoes, and broth and bring to a boil. Lower the heat to a simmer and stir in the black beans, kidney beans, half of the pinto beans, and the chiles. Season with salt and pepper to taste and simmer for 15 to 20 minutes to allow the flavors to blend.

While the soup is simmering, puree the remaining pinto beans in a blender or food processor until smooth, adding a little of the hot soup broth if needed to make it smooth and creamy. Scrape the pureed bean mixture into the soup, along with the hot sauce and liquid smoke, stirring to combine. Taste and adjust the seasonings, if needed. Serve hot.

zucchini and white bean soup

serves 4

White beans add protein and creaminess to this tasty soup made with zucchini and garnished with chopped fresh tomato. When you wash the zucchini, be sure to scrub it well to remove any bits of dirt.

1 tablespoon olive oil or ¼ cup water
1 medium yellow onion, chopped
1 pound zucchini, trimmed
    and coarsely chopped
3 or 4 cloves garlic, minced
½ teaspoon dried oregano
4 cups vegetable broth

1½ cups home-cooked white beans, or
    1 (15.5-ounce) can, drained and rinsed
1 (14.5-ounce) can diced
    fire-roasted tomatoes, drained
Salt and freshly ground black pepper
⅓ cup chopped fresh basil
¼ cup chopped fresh tomato

Heat the oil in a large saucepan over medium-high heat. Add the onion and cook until softened, 5 minutes. Add the zucchini and garlic and cook for 3 minutes longer. Stir in the oregano, broth, white beans, tomatoes, and salt and pepper to taste. Bring to a boil, then lower the heat to a simmer and cook until the vegetables are tender, about 15 minutes.

Add the basil, then taste and adjust the seasonings, if needed. Serve hot, topped with the chopped tomato.

hummus soup with pita croutons

serves 4

All the flavors you love in a good hummus are combined to make a great-tasting soup, made even more special with the addition of crunchy pita croutons. This rich and flavorful soup makes four small servings. For larger servings, double the recipe.

2 pita loaves
Olive oil (optional)
Salt
1½ cups home-cooked chickpeas, or
   1 (15.5-ounce) can, drained and rinsed
2 cloves garlic, chopped
½ teaspoon ground cumin

⅛ teaspoon cayenne
2 tablespoons sesame tahini
2 tablespoons freshly
   squeezed lemon juice
2 cups vegetable broth
2 tablespoons minced fresh
   Italian parsley or cilantro

Preheat the oven to 350°F. Carefully slice each pita bread into two circles with a serrated knife. Lightly brush olive oil, if using, onto the inner side of each circle. Cut the pita circles into 1-inch strips, then stack the strips and cut them into 1-inch squares. Arrange the pieces on a baking sheet in a single layer, oil side up. Sprinkle with salt to taste. Bake until golden brown, about 10 minutes. Set aside.

In a high-speed blender or food processor, combine the chickpeas, garlic, cumin, cayenne, and ¼ teaspoon of salt. Process until finely minced. Add the tahini, lemon juice, and broth and process until smooth, scraping down as needed. Taste and adjust the seasonings. If serving at room temperature, transfer the soup to bowls; if serving warm, transfer to a saucepan and heat gently over low heat, stirring, until just hot, then transfer to bowls; if serving chilled, refrigerate for 1 to 2 hours, then transfer to bowls. Garnish with the pita croutons and parsley.

guacamole soup

serves 4

The first time I made this creamy chilled soup, I simply thinned out some leftover guacamole with a little vegetable broth. The result was so good that I decided it should have its own recipe. This soup can be enjoyed right away but is best served chilled, so if you want to serve it right after you make it, have all your ingredients chilled. Otherwise, you may want to allow for some time in the fridge before serving. This soup is best served within a few hours after it is made, but the flavor does benefit from an hour or two in the refrigerator. If you prefer a thinner soup, stir in a little extra plain unsweetened almond milk just before serving.

2 Hass avocados
2 scallions, chopped
1½ cups vegetable broth
½ cup plain unsweetened almond
   milk or other nondairy milk
½ cup vegan sour cream
2 tablespoons freshly squeezed lime juice

¼ teaspoon ground cumin
¼ teaspoon chili powder
¼ teaspoon smoked paprika (optional)
½ teaspoon salt
¼ teaspoon freshly ground black pepper
½ cup chopped fresh tomato
   or tomato salsa

Halve and pit the avocados. Scoop out the flesh with a spoon and chop.

In a high-speed blender or food processor, combine the avocados, scallions, broth, almond milk, sour cream, lime juice, cumin, chili powder, paprika, if using, salt, and pepper. Blend until smooth, then transfer to a bowl. Serve as is or refrigerate for 1 to 2 hours to serve chilled. If you prefer a thinner soup, stir in a little extra almond milk or broth. When ready to serve, transfer the soup to bowls and top with the chopped tomato.

succotash soup

serves 4

Corn and lima beans, the key ingredients of succotash, combine in this summer-kissed soup. Instead of limas, you can substitute edamame or butter beans. If fresh corn is out of season, try frozen corn kernels instead. I use Better Than Bouillon brand vegetable soup base whenever I don't have homemade broth on hand.

1 tablespoon olive oil or ¼ cup water
1 large yellow onion, chopped
1 celery rib, chopped
3 cloves garlic, minced
2½ cups fresh or frozen baby lima beans
   or shelled butter beans or edamame
5 cups vegetable broth

3 cups fresh corn kernels (from about
   6 ears of corn) or frozen corn kernels
Salt and freshly ground black pepper
1 large fresh tomato, chopped
1 tablespoon minced fresh Italian
   parsley, basil, or dill

Heat the oil in a large pot over medium-high heat. Add the onion, celery, and garlic and cook for 5 minutes to soften. Stir in the lima beans and broth and bring to a boil. Lower the heat to a simmer and cook for 10 minutes. Stir in the corn kernels and cook for 5 minutes longer, until the vegetables are tender. Season with salt and pepper to taste.

Transfer about 2 cups of the soup to a blender or food processor and process until smooth. Stir the mixture back into the soup. Taste and adjust the seasonings. To serve, ladle into bowls and top each serving with the chopped tomato and parsley.

garden vegetable bean soup

serves 4

It's easy to enjoy homemade vegetable soup in 30 minutes. The trick is cutting your vegetables thinly so they take less time to cook. I usually chop the vegetables that go in first and get them started cooking, then cut the rest and add them. If you're really in a time squeeze, you could buy pre-chopped veggies at the supermarket. If you don't have cooked grains or pasta on hand, you can add some uncooked quick-cooking rice, quinoa, or pasta to the pot when you add the broth and cook until tender.

1 tablespoon olive oil or ¼ cup water
1 medium yellow onion, minced
1 medium carrot, thinly sliced
3 cloves garlic, minced
6 cups vegetable broth
1½ cups home-cooked cannellini
    beans, or 1 (15.5-ounce) can,
    drained and rinsed
1 medium zucchini, coarsely chopped

1 teaspoon salt
½ teaspoon dried marjoram
¼ teaspoon freshly ground black pepper
4 cups chopped kale
1 large fresh tomato, chopped
2 tablespoons minced fresh
    Italian parsley or basil
1 cup cooked brown rice, quinoa,
    or small-shape pasta

Heat the oil in a large pot over medium heat. Add the onion, carrot, and garlic. Cover and cook for 5 minutes to soften. Stir in the broth, beans, zucchini, salt, marjoram, and pepper. Bring to a boil, then lower the heat to a simmer and cook until the vegetables are tender, about 10 minutes. Stir in the kale, chopped tomato, and parsley and cook for 5 minutes longer. Stir in the cooked rice. Taste and adjust the seasonings, if needed. Serve hot.

french white bean soup

serves 4

Creamy cannellini beans are always my first choice when it comes to white beans. They're large enough to sink your teeth into, with a great texture and flavor. If unavailable, you can substitute another white bean, such as navy or Great Northerns.

1 tablespoon olive oil or ¼ cup water
1 large yellow onion, minced
1 carrot, minced
1 celery rib, minced
1 medium Yukon Gold potato,
    peeled and chopped
3 cloves garlic, minced
2 teaspoons dried herbes de Provence

2 bay leaves
3 cups home-cooked cannellini beans, or
    2 (15.5-ounce) cans, drained and rinsed
5 cups vegetable broth
Salt and freshly ground black pepper
½ teaspoon smoked paprika
½ teaspoon liquid smoke (optional)
4 tablespoons vegan sour cream

Heat the oil in a large pot over medium heat. Add the onion, carrot, celery, potato, and garlic. Cover and cook until softened, 5 minutes. Stir in the herbes de Provence, then add the bay leaves, beans, broth, and salt and pepper to taste. Bring to a boil, then lower the heat to medium and simmer until the vegetables are tender, about 15 minutes.

Remove the bay leaves and stir in the paprika and liquid smoke, if using. Puree about half of the soup in a blender or food processor, then return it to the pot; or use an immersion blender to puree it right in the pot. Taste and adjust the seasonings, if needed. To serve, ladle the hot soup into bowls and top each serving with a tablespoon of sour cream.

harissa-spiked pumpkin soup

serves 4

The fiery Tunisian chile paste known as harissa adds heat and depth of flavor to this soup. Harissa is available in the gourmet section of supermarkets or online. A recipe for harissa follows, if you prefer to make your own.

1 tablespoon olive oil or ¼ cup water
1 medium yellow onion, finely chopped
1 teaspoon grated fresh ginger
1 (15-ounce) can solid-pack pumpkin
1 (14.5-ounce) can diced
    tomatoes, including juices
1 tablespoon harissa (recipe
    follows), plus more for serving

3 cups vegetable broth
Salt and freshly ground black pepper
¼ cup coarsely chopped toasted
    almonds or hazelnuts
2 tablespoons chopped fresh
    Italian parsley or cilantro

Heat the oil in a large pot over medium heat. Add the onion, cover, and cook until softened, 5 minutes. Stir in the ginger, pumpkin, tomatoes, and harissa, stirring to blend. Stir in the broth and season with salt and pepper to taste. Bring to a boil, then lower the heat to medium and simmer for 10 minutes or until the flavors are well combined. Taste and adjust the seasonings, if needed. Serve hot, topped with the almonds and parsley. Place a small bowl of extra harissa on the table for those who wish to add more.

harissa
makes about 1 cup

1 ounce dried hot chiles, stemmed,
    seeded, and broken into pieces
1 ounce dried mild chiles, stemmed,
    seeded, and broken into pieces
1 roasted red bell pepper, blotted dry
2 cloves garlic, crushed
1 teaspoon ground caraway seeds
1 teaspoon ground coriander
1 teaspoon salt
½ teaspoon ground cumin
Olive oil, for topping

Combine the hot and mild chiles in a heatproof bowl and cover with boiling water. Set aside for 30 minutes, then drain well and transfer to a food processor. Add all of the remaining ingredients and process to a paste. If the mixture is too thick, add a small amount of olive oil. Transfer to a bowl or a jar with a tight-fitting lid and top with a thin layer of olive oil. Cover tightly and refrigerate until needed. Properly stored, it will keep well for 1 week in the refrigerator or up to 3 months in the freezer.

black bean–pumpkin soup

serves 4

Canned pumpkin adds richness and depth of flavor to hearty black bean soup. This thick and delicious soup makes a quick and easy meal accompanied by a green salad and warm corn bread. For a creamier soup, puree all or part of the soup in a blender or food processor or right in the pot using an immersion blender.

1 tablespoon olive oil or ¼ cup water
1 medium yellow onion, finely chopped
3 cloves garlic, minced
3 cups home-cooked black beans, or
    2 (15.5-ounce) cans, drained and rinsed
1 (15-ounce) can solid-pack pumpkin
3 cups vegetable broth

1 teaspoon ground cumin
½ teaspoon dried oregano
Salt and freshly ground black pepper
1 teaspoon liquid smoke (optional)
3 tablespoons minced scallions
    or fresh cilantro

Heat the oil in a large pot over medium heat. Add the onion and garlic and cook until softened, about 5 minutes. Stir in the beans, pumpkin, broth, cumin, oregano, and salt and pepper to taste. Bring to a boil, then lower the heat to medium and simmer until the flavors are blended, about 10 minutes. When ready to serve, stir in the liquid smoke, if using, and the scallions.

smoky corn chowder

serves 4 to 6

Frozen corn kernels are used to make this soup instead of fresh corn because the frozen variety saves preparation time and is always available. This rich chowder gets its smoky accents from smoked paprika, liquid smoke, and the optional vegan bacon garnish.

1 tablespoon olive oil or ¼ cup water
1 large yellow onion, chopped
1 celery rib, thinly sliced
1 Yukon Gold potato, peeled
   and chopped
2 cups vegetable broth
1 (16-ounce) package frozen
   corn kernels, thawed
½ teaspoon smoked paprika
Salt and freshly ground black pepper

1 (16-ounce) can creamed corn
½ cup plain unsweetened almond
   milk or other nondairy milk
1 teaspoon liquid smoke
2 slices vegan bacon, cooked
   and chopped (optional)
2 teaspoons chopped pickled
   jalapeño chiles
2 tablespoons chopped fresh
   cilantro or Italian parsley

Heat the oil in a large pot over medium-high heat. Add the onion, celery, and potato. Cover and cook until softened, about 5 minutes. Stir in the vegetable broth and bring to a boil. Lower the heat to medium and add the thawed corn kernels, paprika, and salt and pepper to taste. Simmer until the vegetables are tender, about 15 minutes.

While the soup is simmering, combine the creamed corn and almond milk in a blender and blend until smooth and creamy, then stir the mixture into the soup along with the liquid smoke. Heat for a minute or two, until hot, then taste and adjust the seasonings, if needed. To serve, ladle into bowls and sprinkle each serving with vegan bacon, if using, jalapeños, and cilantro.

lemony chickpea-spinach soup

serves 4

Deliciously satisfying yet refreshingly light, this soup seasoned with oregano, lemon juice, and kalamata olives sparkles with the flavors of the Greek islands. It is equally good made with couscous or with cooked rice or quinoa, if you have some on hand.

1 tablespoon olive oil or ¼ cup water
1 medium yellow onion, finely chopped
2 cloves garlic, minced
1½ cups home-cooked chickpeas, or
    1 (15.5-ounce) can, drained and rinsed
½ teaspoon dried oregano
4 cups vegetable broth
6 cups coarsely chopped fresh spinach

Salt and freshly ground black pepper
½ cup dried (uncooked) couscous or
    1½ cups cooked brown rice or quinoa
2 to 3 tablespoons freshly
    squeezed lemon juice (preferably
    from Meyer lemons)
¼ cup kalamata olives,
    pitted and chopped

Heat the oil in a large pot over medium heat. Add the onion and garlic, cover, and cook until softened, 5 minutes. Add the chickpeas, oregano, and broth and bring to a boil, then lower the heat to medium and simmer for 5 minutes. Stir in the spinach and season with salt and pepper to taste. Add the couscous and cook for 5 minutes longer. Stir in the lemon juice, then taste and adjust the seasonings, if needed. To serve, ladle into bowls and top with the chopped olives.

creamy tomato soup

serves 4 to 6

Fire-roasted tomatoes add an extra layer of flavor, while white beans contribute protein and creaminess to this delicious soup that is worlds away from the "kid's stuff" brand of tomato soup many of us grew up eating.

1 tablespoon olive oil or ¼ cup water
1 medium yellow onion, minced
1 carrot, shredded
3 cloves garlic, minced
1 teaspoon dried basil
½ teaspoon dried oregano or marjoram
¼ teaspoon cayenne (optional)
2 (28-ounce) cans fire-roasted
   tomatoes, including juices

1½ cups home-cooked white beans, or
   1 (15.5-ounce) can, drained and rinsed
2 cups vegetable broth
½ teaspoon salt
¼ teaspoon freshly ground black pepper
Pinch or two of natural sugar (optional)
Fresh basil leaves, for garnish

Heat the oil in a large pot over medium heat. Add the onion, carrot, and garlic. Cover and cook until softened, 5 minutes. Stir in the basil, oregano, and cayenne, if using, then add the tomatoes, white beans, broth, salt, and pepper. Bring to a boil, then lower the heat to medium and simmer until the vegetables are tender, about 10 minutes.

Transfer the soup, in batches if needed, to a high-speed blender or food processor and process until smooth and creamy. Return the soup to the pot and taste and adjust the seasonings, if needed. If it tastes too tart, add a pinch or two of sugar to balance the flavor. If the soup is too thick, stir in a bit more vegetable broth. Serve hot, garnished with fresh basil.

clear shiitake soup
with bok choy and edamame

serves 4

Typical of Japanese-style soups, this is a delicate soup with a light broth. The chewy shiitakes and edamame add substance. If you prefer a heartier soup, you can also add some diced tofu and/or some cooked brown rice.

8 ounces shiitake mushrooms,
   stemmed and sliced
1 medium head bok choy,
   chopped (about 6 cups)
1 cup fresh or frozen shelled edamame
2 teaspoons grated fresh ginger

6 cups vegetable broth
⅓ cup white miso paste
5 scallions, minced
1 tablespoon mirin
1 tablespoon tamari soy sauce

In a large pot, combine the mushrooms, bok choy, edamame, ginger, and broth and bring to a boil. Lower the heat to medium and simmer for 10 minutes to blend the flavors. Remove about 1 cup of the broth and blend it in a bowl with the miso paste until smooth. Stir the miso mixture back into the pot. Do not boil. Add the scallions, mirin, and tamari. Taste and adjust the seasonings, if needed. Serve hot.

thai coconut soup with tofu

serves 4

For a spicy soup, stir in 1 teaspoon or more of Asian chili paste or add a minced hot chile when you add the red bell pepper. You can also put a condiment tray on the table containing bowls of hot red pepper flakes, lime wedges, soy sauce, and bean sprouts for people to add to their bowls as desired.

1 red bell pepper, stemmed, seeded, and chopped
1 small carrot, coarsely grated
5 scallions, minced
2 teaspoons grated fresh ginger
3 cups vegetable broth
2 tablespoons tamari soy sauce

8 ounces extra-firm tofu, cut into ½-inch dice
1 (13.5-ounce) can unsweetened coconut milk
½ cup frozen baby peas
1 tablespoon freshly squeezed lime juice
½ cup chopped fresh cilantro or Thai basil leaves

In a large pot, combine the bell pepper, carrot, scallions, and ginger. Stir in the broth and bring to a boil. Lower the heat to a simmer and cook for 5 minutes. Stir in the tamari, tofu, coconut milk, and peas and cook for 3 minutes. Do not boil. Stir in the lime juice, then taste and adjust the seasonings, if needed. To serve, ladle into bowls and top with the cilantro.

chipotle–sweet potato bisque

serves 4

This velvety soup has a stunning color and flavor thanks to the combination of sweet potatoes and chipotle chiles. Enriched with white beans, it's also very satisfying. Add your favorite cooked vegetable to the pureed soup—some chopped kale or spinach would be especially good.

1 tablespoon olive oil or ¼ cup water
1 medium yellow onion, finely chopped
1 large or 2 medium sweet potatoes, chopped (about 3 cups)
1 (14-ounce) can fire-roasted diced tomatoes, including juices
1½ cups home-cooked white beans, or 1 (15.5-ounce) can, drained and rinsed

2 tablespoons canned chipotle chiles in adobo
2 tablespoons tamari soy sauce
4 cups vegetable broth
Salt and freshly ground black pepper
1 tablespoon minced fresh chives or Italian parsley

Heat the oil or water in a large pot over medium heat. Add the onion and sweet potatoes. Cover and cook until softened, 5 minutes. Stir in the tomatoes, white beans, chipotle chiles, and tamari.

Add the broth and season with salt and pepper to taste. Bring to a boil, then decrease the heat to low and simmer until the vegetables are tender, about 12 minutes. Use an immersion blender to puree the soup right in the pot, or transfer the soup to a blender or food processor and process until smooth, then return to the pot. Reheat, if needed. Serve hot, sprinkled with the chives.

green chile stew (caldillo)

serves 4 or 5

Roasted green chiles play the starring role in this hearty Mexican stew known as caldillo. Buying roasted green chiles in a jar will make this soup ready in no time. (If you can find fire-roasted green chiles, it's even better!) If you prefer to roast your own, follow the guidelines on page 20.

1 tablespoon olive oil or ¼ cup water
1 large yellow onion, chopped
4 large cloves garlic, minced
1½ pounds Yukon Gold potatoes, peeled and chopped
2 (14.5-ounce) cans diced fire-roasted tomatoes, including juices

1 (8-ounce) jar roasted mild green chiles, drained and chopped
4 cups vegetable broth
2 cups diced seitan or reconstituted soy curls
1 teaspoon ground cumin
Salt and freshly ground black pepper
½ cup chopped fresh cilantro

Heat the oil in a soup pot over medium-high heat. Add the onion, garlic, and potatoes. Cover and cook, stirring occasionally, for 5 minutes or until the vegetables soften. Add the tomatoes, chiles, and broth. Bring to a boil, then lower the heat to a simmer and add the seitan, cumin, and salt and pepper to taste. Cover and cook until the vegetables are tender, about 15 minutes. Stir in the cilantro and serve hot.

big
bowls

The recipes in this chapter are among my favorites in the book, probably because I love the casual comfort that bowl food delivers. These recipes are essentially one-dish meals designed to be eaten in—you guessed it—a big bowl. Quick and easy to assemble and a delight to eat, the big bowls in this chapter include fresh takes on favorite dishes with Sushi Bowls (page 48), Mac UnCheesy Bowls (page 58), and even Tempeh Reuben Bowls (page 61). From Balti Bowls (page 54) and Tempeh Larb (page 57) to Chimichurri Quinoa Bowls (page 56) and Mediterranean Tofu Scram-Bowls (page 64), these recipes hail from all over the world. What they all have in common is that they are complete, balanced meals that include lots of vegetables, grains, and plant proteins. What else do these recipes have in common? They're 100 percent delicious and can be ready to eat in 30 minutes. Bring on the big bowls!

quinoa and chickpeas
with arugula pesto

serves 4

This assertive pesto made with arugula and walnuts is a delicious way to enliven quinoa. Studded with chickpeas, artichoke hearts, tomatoes, and olives, this is a sublime meal in a bowl.

1 cup quinoa, well rinsed and drained
2 cups water or vegetable broth
Salt
½ cup toasted walnut pieces
2 cloves garlic, crushed
2 cups packed arugula
¼ cup olive oil
1 tablespoon freshly
   squeezed lemon juice

¼ teaspoon freshly ground black pepper
1½ cups home-cooked chickpeas, or
   1 (15.5-ounce) can, drained and rinsed
1 cup canned artichoke hearts, chopped
1 cup chopped fresh tomatoes
¼ cup kalamata olives,
   pitted and chopped

Combine the quinoa and water in a saucepan and add salt. Cover and bring to a boil. Lower the heat to a simmer and cook, covered, for 15 to 20 minutes.

While the quinoa is cooking, combine the walnuts and garlic in a food processor and finely chop. Add the arugula, olive oil, lemon juice, ½ teaspoon salt, and the pepper. Blend until smooth.

When the quinoa is tender, stir in the chickpeas, artichoke hearts, tomatoes, olives, and about ½ cup of the pesto. Toss gently to combine. Taste and adjust the seasonings, adding more pesto or salt, if needed.

romesco vegetable bowls

serves 4

Creamy romesco sauce tops a flavorful array of roasted vegetables and chickpeas, surrounded by wedges of warm pita bread. Using jarred roasted red peppers for the sauce cuts down on prep time, but if you have home-roasted peppers on hand, use them instead. Also, if you have some roasted garlic already prepared, use it instead of raw garlic in the sauce for extra flavor.

2 portobello mushroom caps, halved, cut into ½-inch slices
1 large yellow bell pepper, seeded and cut into 1-inch pieces
1 eggplant, trimmed and cut into ½-inch dice
1 medium zucchini, trimmed and cut into ½-inch dice
3 small shallots, quartered
1½ cups home-cooked chickpeas, or 1 (15.5-ounce) can, drained and rinsed
1 tablespoon olive oil

1½ teaspoons smoked paprika
Salt and freshly ground black pepper
½ cup blanched almonds
1 (8-ounce) jar roasted red bell peppers or 2 red bell peppers, roasted and seeded
1 to 2 cloves garlic, chopped
2 fresh plum tomatoes, chopped
2 tablespoons oil-packed or reconstituted sun-dried tomatoes
1½ tablespoons sherry vinegar
Warm pita bread, for serving

Preheat the oven to 425°F. Spray a large baking sheet (or two) with nonstick cooking spray. Combine the mushrooms, yellow bell pepper, eggplant, zucchini, shallots, and chickpeas on the baking sheet. Drizzle with the olive oil and sprinkle with ½ teaspoon of the paprika and salt and pepper to taste. Toss to coat, then spread the vegetables in a single layer. Roast until the vegetables are tender inside and nicely browned, 20 to 25 minutes, turning once about halfway through.

While the vegetables are roasting, grind the almonds to a paste in a high-speed blender or food processor. Add the roasted red bell peppers, garlic, plum tomatoes, sun-dried tomatoes, vinegar, the remaining 1 teaspoon paprika, ½ teaspoon salt, and ¼ teaspoon black pepper. Blend until smooth and creamy. Taste and adjust the seasonings, if needed. The sauce should be thick and creamy. Transfer the sauce to a small saucepan and heat gently over low heat. Add a little water if the sauce is too thick.

To serve, spoon the vegetables into bowls and spoon the sauce on top. Serve hot with the pita bread.

greens and black-eyed peas with smoky grits

serves 4

Two Southern favorites, grits and black-eyed peas, team up for this delectable meal in a bowl. The time is kept to a minimum with quick-cooking grits, so if all you have is regular grits, it will take longer to cook. If grits are unavailable, substitute quick-cooking polenta. I especially like kale in this dish, but you can use other greens instead.

1 cup quick-cooking or regular grits
1 teaspoon liquid smoke
Salt and freshly ground black pepper
1 tablespoon olive oil
1 medium onion, chopped
2 cloves garlic, minced

9 ounces kale, coarsely chopped
½ cup vegetable broth
½ teaspoon smoked paprika
1½ cups home-cooked black-eyed peas, or 1 (15.5-ounce) can, drained and rinsed

Cook the grits according to the package directions. (It should take about 5 minutes for quick-cooking grits and 20 to 25 minutes for regular grits to cook.) Stir in the liquid smoke and salt and pepper to taste and keep warm.

Heat the oil in a large skillet over medium heat. Add the onion and garlic, cover, and cook until softened, about 5 minutes. Add the kale, broth, and paprika and season with salt and pepper to taste. Cook, stirring to wilt the kale, then stir in the black-eyed peas and continue to cook until tender, about 10 minutes. Taste and adjust the seasonings, if needed. To serve, top the grits with the kale mixture.

sushi bowls

serves 4

Inspired by the Japanese dish known as chirashi zushi, or "scattered sushi," these bowls contain the same delicious flavor and ingredients of sushi but without all the fuss.

3 to 4 cups cooked sushi rice or
  brown rice, at room temperature
2 teaspoons rice vinegar
1 teaspoon agave nectar
½ teaspoon sea salt
1 English cucumber, peeled
  and cut into matchsticks
1 red bell pepper, stemmed, seeded,
  and cut into matchsticks
1 carrot, finely shredded
1 tablespoon tamari soy sauce
1 teaspoon toasted sesame oil

1 (8-ounce) package baked marinated
  tofu, cut into thin strips
1 Hass avocado, pitted, peeled,
  and cut into ½-inch dice
1 or 2 (7 by 8-inch) sheets dried nori,
  cut into ¼-inch squares or torn
  into small pieces (see Note)
3 scallions, thinly sliced
1 tablespoon toasted sesame seeds
Tamari, wasabi paste, pickled ginger,
  and seasoned rice vinegar, for serving

Place the cooked rice in a bowl. Add the vinegar, agave, and salt and toss gently to combine. Set aside.

In a medium bowl, combine the cucumber, bell pepper, and carrot. Add the tamari and sesame oil and toss to coat.

Divide the rice among serving bowls. Top each portion with the vegetable mixture, dividing evenly. Arrange the tofu strips on top of the vegetables and top with the avocado. Scatter the nori, scallions, and sesame seeds among the bowls. Serve with additional tamari, wasabi, pickled ginger, and seasoned rice vinegar for diners to use as desired.

note: Use sharp scissors to quickly and easily cut nori into uniform pieces, first cutting the sheet into ¼-inch strips, and then stacking the strips and cutting them into ¼-inch pieces.

cannellini spezzatino

serves 4

The classic Italian stew known as spezzatino is traditionally made with beef, but this version features cannellini beans. It's also terrific made with seitan. For a variation, you can leave out the potatoes and serve it over warm polenta.

1 tablespoon olive oil or ¼ cup water
1 large yellow onion, chopped
2 carrots, thinly sliced
2 Yukon Gold potatoes, cut
   into ½-inch dice
1 celery rib, thinly sliced
3 cloves garlic, run through a garlic press
3 tablespoons tomato paste
1 teaspoon dried marjoram
½ teaspoon dried oregano
1 teaspoon salt

½ teaspoon freshly ground black pepper
½ cup dry white wine (optional)
1 (14.5-ounce) can diced
   tomatoes, including juices
1½ to 2 cups vegetable broth
1 bay leaf
1½ cups home-cooked cannellini
   beans, or 1 (15.5-ounce) can,
   rinsed and drained
4 cups chopped Tuscan kale or spinach
½ cup chopped fresh basil leaves

In a large pot, heat the oil over medium-high heat. Add the onion, carrots, potatoes, celery, and garlic. Cover and cook until the vegetables are softened, stirring occasionally, about 5 minutes. Stir in the tomato paste, marjoram, oregano, salt, and pepper. Stir in the wine, if using. Add the tomatoes, broth, and bay leaf and bring to a boil. Lower the heat to medium, stir in the cannellini beans, and simmer, uncovered, for 15 minutes.

Remove the bay leaf and discard. Stir in the kale and basil and cook for 4 minutes longer to wilt the kale. Taste and adjust the seasonings, if needed.

banh-mi bowls

serves 4

I so much enjoy the Vietnamese sandwich known as banh-mi that the flavors and textures have inspired me to create other dishes with the theme. So far I've made a banh-mi salad, a pizza, and also the delicious noodle dish on page 111. My latest inspiration is this banh-mi dinner bowl featuring toasted croutons to soak up the delicious sauce and stand in for the sandwich bread. For convenience, packaged baked marinated tofu is the protein of choice, but you can instead use your own homemade Baked Marinated Tofu (page 15) or Seitan Trio (page 14). Instead of using the bread, this is also terrific served over cooked brown rice.

4 (½-inch-thick) slices Italian bread
   or 8 slices French baguette
1 large carrot, finely shredded
½ English cucumber, peeled,
   seeded, and chopped
2 cups finely shredded cabbage
1 cup fresh cilantro leaves
1 teaspoon toasted sesame oil
1 tablespoon neutral vegetable oil
2 cloves garlic, minced

¼ cup minced scallions
1½ teaspoons grated fresh ginger
1 (8-ounce) package baked
   tofu, cut into thin strips
3 tablespoons tamari soy sauce
3 tablespoons hoisin sauce
1 to 2 teaspoons sriracha sauce
1 teaspoon natural sugar
2 tablespoons rice vinegar

Preheat the broiler. Arrange the bread slices on a baking sheet and toast under the broiler on both sides, turning once. Remove from the oven and cut the toasted bread into 1-inch pieces. Set aside.

In a large bowl, combine the carrot, cucumber, cabbage, and cilantro. Drizzle on the sesame oil and toss gently to combine. Divide the vegetable mixture among serving bowls and set aside.

Heat the vegetable oil in a medium skillet over medium heat. Add the garlic, scallions, and ginger and cook for 1 minute. Add the tofu and 1 tablespoon of the tamari and mix well to coat the tofu. Set aside to cool.

In a small bowl, combine the remaining 2 tablespoons tamari with the hoisin, sriracha, sugar, and vinegar, stirring well to blend. Arrange the reserved toasted bread on top of the vegetables in the bowls. Top with the tofu mixture and drizzle each bowl with the sauce.

roasted vegetable tabouli bowls

serves 4

This twist on the classic Middle Eastern bulgur salad is topped with colorful roasted vegetables that provide deep and delicious flavor notes. It's a deceptively quick and easy meal in a bowl.

3 shallots, thinly sliced
1 large yellow bell pepper,
    seeded and cut into strips
2 cups cherry tomatoes, halved
Salt and freshly ground black pepper
1 cup medium-grind bulgur
3 tablespoons olive oil
2 tablespoons freshly
    squeezed lemon juice

1½ cups home-cooked cannellini
    beans, or 1 (15.5-ounce) can,
    rinsed and drained
½ cucumber, peeled, seeded,
    and chopped
¾ cup minced fresh Italian parsley leaves
2 tablespoons minced scallions

Preheat the oven to 425°F. Arrange the shallots, bell pepper, and tomatoes in a lightly oiled baking pan. Season with ½ teaspoon salt and ¼ teaspoon pepper. Roast the vegetables until tender, 12 to 15 minutes. Remove from the oven and set aside.

In the meantime, bring 1½ cups water to a boil in a saucepan. Add the bulgur and salt to taste. Remove from the heat, cover, and set aside for 15 minutes.

In a small bowl, whisk together the olive oil, lemon juice, and salt and pepper to taste until blended.

Transfer the softened bulgur to a large bowl. Add the beans, cucumber, parsley, and scallions. Pour the dressing over the salad and toss well to combine. Divide the mixture among shallow serving bowls. Top with the roasted vegetables and serve.

moroccan couscous bowls

serves 4

In just minutes, you can be enjoying a bowl filled with colorful vegetables, fragrant spices, and satisfying chickpeas and couscous, finished with a crunch of almonds. So what are you waiting for?

1 tablespoon olive oil or ¼ cup water
1 small red onion, chopped
1 red bell pepper, finely chopped
1 large carrot, shredded
1 teaspoon grated fresh ginger
¾ teaspoon ground coriander
¾ teaspoon ground cumin
⅛ teaspoon ground cinnamon
1½ cups vegetable broth
1½ cups home-cooked chickpeas, or
   1 (15.5-ounce) can, rinsed and drained

1 cup couscous
1 cup frozen green peas, thawed
½ cup golden raisins or
   chopped dried apricots
1 tablespoon freshly
   squeezed lemon juice
Salt and freshly ground black pepper
¼ cup chopped fresh Italian
   parsley or cilantro
¼ cup toasted slivered almonds

Heat the oil in a large pot over medium heat. Add the onion and bell pepper and cook until softened, about 5 minutes. Add the carrot, ginger, coriander, cumin, and cinnamon. Stir in the broth, cover, and bring to a boil. Lower the heat to a simmer, stir in the chickpeas, and simmer for 5 minutes. Stir in the couscous, peas, raisins, and lemon juice. Season with salt and pepper to taste. Remove from the heat, cover, and set aside for 5 minutes. When ready to serve, add the parsley and fluff with a fork. Divide among serving bowls, and sprinkle with the almonds.

quinoa and black bean chili bowls

serves 4

This bowl has multiple layers of flavor and texture built in, from nutty quinoa and creamy black beans to smoky-hot chipotle chiles and sweet bursts of corn kernels. You can add even more deliciousness with the optional avocado, sour cream, and cilantro. If you're not a fan of heat, you can cut back on or omit the chipotles and use less chili powder.

1 tablespoon olive oil or ¼ cup water
1 medium yellow onion, chopped
1 small red bell pepper, seeded and chopped
3 cloves garlic, minced
1 to 2 tablespoons minced canned chipotle chiles in adobo
1 to 2 tablespoons chili powder
½ teaspoon dried oregano
½ teaspoon ground cumin
¾ cup quinoa, well rinsed and drained
1 cup vegetable broth or water

1 (14.5-ounce) can fire-roasted diced tomatoes, including juices
3 cups home-cooked black beans, or 2 (15.5-ounce) cans, rinsed and drained
1 cup frozen corn kernels
2 cups finely chopped fresh spinach, chard, or kale
Salt and freshly ground black pepper
1 Hass avocado (optional)
½ cup vegan sour cream (optional)
2 tablespoons chopped fresh cilantro (optional)

Heat the oil in a large pot over medium heat. Add the onion, bell pepper, and garlic. Cover and cook until softened, about 5 minutes. Stir in the chipotle chiles, chili powder, oregano, cumin, quinoa, and broth. Add the tomatoes and bring to a boil. Lower the heat to a simmer, cover, and cook for 15 minutes. Add the beans, corn, spinach, and salt and pepper to taste. Simmer, uncovered, for 10 minutes longer, stirring occasionally. Taste and adjust the seasonings, if needed.

To serve, halve and pit the avocado. Scoop out the flesh with a spoon and chop. Transfer the quinoa mixture to serving bowls and serve hot, topped with the sour cream, cilantro, and avocado, if using.

balti bowls

serves 4

This recipe gets its name from a curry dish popular in Great Britain that is traditionally served in a steel bowl similar to a wok called a "balti bowl." Naan bread or other Indian flatbreads can be found in well-stocked supermarkets. If you prefer to skip the naan, you can serve this over hot cooked basmati rice instead.

1 tablespoon olive oil
1 medium yellow onion, coarsely grated
2 cloves garlic, minced
1 small fresh green chile, seeded and chopped
2 teaspoons finely grated fresh ginger
2 teaspoons garam masala
1 teaspoon ground cumin
1 teaspoon ground coriander
2 tablespoons tomato paste

1 (14.5-ounce) can diced tomatoes, including juices
1 teaspoon salt
2 cups diced seitan, extra-firm tofu, cooked or canned chickpeas, or reconstituted soy curls
3 cups coarsely chopped fresh spinach
2 tablespoons chopped fresh cilantro
Plain vegan yogurt, for serving
Mango chutney, for serving
Warm naan or basmati rice, for serving

Heat the oil in a large pot or deep skillet over medium-high heat. Add the onion, garlic, chile, and ginger and cook for 4 minutes or until the onion starts to turn golden. Lower the heat to medium and stir in the garam masala, cumin, and coriander. Stir in the tomato paste, then add the tomatoes and salt and cook for 3 minutes. Stir in the seitan, then add the spinach, stirring to wilt. If the sauce is too thick, stir in a small amount of water to achieve the desired consistency. Garnish with the cilantro, and serve with the yogurt, chutney, and naan.

red beans and sweet potato with watercress and walnuts

serves 4

The vibrant colors of the ingredients in this recipe resemble autumn in a bowl. And it tastes delicious thanks to an intriguing combination of textures and flavors. Vary the flavor profile by substituting butternut squash for the sweet potato or a different type of bean for the kidney beans, or by swapping out the watercress for spinach, chard, or kale.

1 large sweet potato, peeled and cut into ½-inch dice

3 cups home-cooked dark red kidney beans, or 2 (15.5-ounce) cans, rinsed and drained

1 bunch fresh watercress, coarsely chopped

½ cup chopped celery

4 scallions, chopped

½ cup toasted walnut pieces

2 tablespoons freshly squeezed lemon juice

1 tablespoon olive oil

1 teaspoon pure maple syrup

1 teaspoon Dijon mustard

Salt and freshly ground black pepper

Steam the diced sweet potato over boiling water until tender, about 10 minutes.

While the sweet potato is steaming, combine the kidney beans, watercress, celery, scallions, walnuts, lemon juice, olive oil, maple syrup, mustard, and salt and pepper to taste in a large bowl. Toss gently to combine. When the sweet potato is cooked, add it to the bowl and toss gently to combine. Taste and adjust the seasonings, if needed. To serve, divide the mixture among serving bowls.

chimichurri quinoa bowls

serves 4

If you love the flavors of garlic, oregano, and parsley, you'll love this bold sauce that hails from Argentina. Since quinoa also hails from South America, the combination seemed like an ideal match. If you enjoy the flavor of cilantro, substitute cilantro for half of the parsley.

1 tablespoon olive oil or ¼ cup water
1 small red onion, chopped
1 small red bell pepper,
   seeded and chopped
1 medium zucchini, diced
¾ cup quinoa, well rinsed and drained
1½ cups water
¾ teaspoon salt
1½ cups home-cooked white beans, or
   1 (15.5-ounce) can, drained and rinsed

4 cloves garlic, crushed
1 cup coarsely chopped
   fresh Italian parsley
1½ teaspoons fresh oregano
   or ½ teaspoon dried
Pinch of natural sugar
½ teaspoon freshly ground black pepper
¼ teaspoon red pepper flakes
1½ tablespoons red wine vinegar
3 tablespoons olive oil

In a large saucepan, heat the 1 tablespoon oil over medium-high heat. Add the onion and bell pepper and sauté for 5 minutes to soften. Stir in the zucchini, quinoa, the 1½ cups water, and ½ teaspoon of the salt. Cover and bring to a boil. Lower the heat to medium and simmer for 10 minutes. Stir in the white beans and continue to cook, covered, until the water is absorbed and the quinoa is tender, about 10 minutes longer. If the liquid is absorbed before the quinoa is tender, add a small amount of extra water.

While the quinoa and vegetables are cooking, combine the garlic, parsley, oregano, sugar, the remaining ¼ teaspoon salt, black pepper, and red pepper flakes in a food processor. Process to a paste, then add the vinegar and the 3 tablespoons oil and process until smooth.

When ready to serve, add as much of the sauce as desired to the quinoa mixture and toss gently to combine. Divide among serving bowls, passing the extra sauce to add as desired.

tempeh larb

serves 4

Traditional Thai larb, or labb, is made with ground meat and served with sticky rice. This version uses tempeh instead of meat and adds the rice directly into the mixture for easy one-bowl servings.

1 pound tempeh, finely chopped
1 tablespoon neutral vegetable oil
2 shallots, thinly sliced
3 tablespoons minced lemongrass,
　　from 1 (3-inch) piece
2 scallions, thinly sliced
½ to 1 teaspoon red pepper flakes
Salt and freshly ground black pepper

⅓ cup freshly squeezed lime juice
3 tablespoons tamari soy sauce
1 tablespoon natural sugar
2 cups cooked brown or jasmine rice
½ cup chopped fresh mint,
　　Thai basil, or cilantro
3 to 4 cups shredded napa cabbage

Steam the tempeh for 15 minutes in a steamer over boiling water.

In a large skillet, heat the oil over medium heat. Add the tempeh, shallots, lemongrass, scallions, red pepper flakes, and salt and pepper to taste. Cook, stirring, for about 5 minutes to soften the shallots and lightly brown the tempeh.

In a small bowl, whisk together the lime juice, tamari, and sugar. Add the dressing to the skillet and cook for 2 minutes. Remove from the heat and stir in the rice and mint. Taste and adjust the seasonings, if needed. To serve, divide the cabbage among serving bowls and divide the tempeh mixture evenly on top.

mac uncheesy bowls

serves 4

If ever there were comfort food in a bowl, it's this recipe. A protein-rich stovetop mac and cheese combines with broccoli for a quick and easy one-dish meal that is sure to please kids of all ages. If preparing this for children, you may want to omit the cayenne. Also, instead of broccoli, you could use a different vegetable, such as chopped spinach or frozen green peas.

8 ounces elbow macaroni
3 cups small broccoli florets
1½ cups home-cooked cannellini
    beans, or 1 (15.5-ounce) can,
    drained and rinsed
¾ cup chopped roasted red bell pepper
    or cooked butternut squash
¾ cup plain unsweetened almond milk or
    other nondairy milk, or more if needed
1 tablespoon tahini
2 tablespoons freshly
    squeezed lemon juice

1 teaspoon yellow mustard
⅓ cup nutritional yeast,
    or more if needed
½ teaspoon smoked paprika
½ teaspoon garlic powder
½ teaspoon onion powder
½ teaspoon dried basil
½ teaspoon salt
¼ teaspoon freshly ground black pepper
Pinch of cayenne or dash of
    hot sauce (optional)

Cook the macaroni in a pot of boiling salted water for 5 minutes. Stir in the broccoli and cook for a few minutes longer, until the pasta is al dente and the broccoli is just tender. Drain and return to the pot.

In a food processor or blender, combine the cannellini beans, bell pepper, almond milk, tahini, lemon juice, mustard, nutritional yeast, paprika, garlic powder, onion powder, basil, salt, and pepper. Add the cayenne, if using. Process until smooth and well blended. Taste and adjust the seasonings, if needed. Add a little more almond milk if the sauce is too thick.

Transfer the sauce mixture to the pot containing the cooked pasta and broccoli. Stir gently over low heat to combine and heat through. To serve, divide the mixture among serving bowls.

sweet potato barbecue bowls

serves 4

Sweet potatoes and pinto beans team up with a smoky barbecue sauce in this lip-smacking bowl of goodness. Use the shredding disk on your food processor to make short work of shredding the sweet potato.

1 tablespoon olive oil or ¼ cup water
½ small red onion, minced
2 cloves garlic, minced
1 large or 2 medium sweet potatoes, peeled and coarsely shredded
1½ cups home-cooked pinto beans, or 1 (15.5-ounce) can, drained and rinsed
2 canned chipotle chiles in adobo, minced
2 tablespoons tomato paste
⅓ cup ketchup

1 tablespoon yellow mustard
1 tablespoon pure maple syrup
1 tablespoon tamari soy sauce
2 teaspoons chili powder
1 teaspoon liquid smoke
½ teaspoon smoked paprika
Salt and freshly ground black pepper
½ cup water
4 cups chopped fresh spinach or baby kale

Heat the oil in a large saucepan over medium heat. Add the onion and garlic and cook until softened, 5 minutes. Stir in the sweet potato, cover, and cook until softened, about 7 minutes, or until tender. Stir in the pinto beans, chipotle chiles, tomato paste, ketchup, mustard, maple syrup, tamari, chili powder, liquid smoke, paprika, and salt and pepper to taste. Stir in as much of the water as needed to make a smooth sauce. Cook, stirring occasionally, to heat through and blend the flavors, about 5 minutes. Stir in the spinach and cook for a few more minutes, until wilted. To serve, divide the mixture evenly among serving bowls.

panzanella bowls

serves 4

This hearty salad features chickpeas, artichoke hearts, black olives, and roasted bell peppers with crisp lettuce and Italian bread in a zesty vinaigrette. It makes a refreshing one-dish meal on days when it's too hot to cook.

5 slices Italian bread, cut into ½-inch dice
1 shallot, chopped
1 clove garlic, chopped
3 tablespoons red wine vinegar
½ teaspoon natural sugar
1 teaspoon chopped fresh oregano
½ teaspoon salt
¼ teaspoon freshly ground black pepper
¼ cup olive oil
1½ cups home-cooked chickpeas, or
   1 (15.5-ounce) can, drained and rinsed

1 large roasted red bell pepper (page
   20), or 1 (6-ounce) jar, well drained
   and blotted dry, cut into 1-inch pieces
1 (6-ounce) jar marinated artichoke
   hearts, drained and quartered
1½ cups grape or cherry tomatoes, halved
⅓ cup brine-cured black olives,
   pitted and halved
1 small head romaine lettuce,
   coarsely chopped
¼ cup chopped fresh Italian
   parsley or basil

Preheat the oven to 375°F. Spread the bread on a baking sheet and bake until lightly toasted, about 12 minutes.

In a blender, combine the shallot, garlic, vinegar, sugar, oregano, salt, and pepper and blend until the shallot and garlic are pureed. Stream in the olive oil and blend until smooth.

In a large bowl, combine the toasted bread cubes, chickpeas, roasted bell pepper, artichoke hearts, tomatoes, olives, lettuce, and parsley. Add the dressing and toss to combine. To serve, divide evenly among serving bowls.

tempeh reuben bowls

serves 4

Just because you may be trying to eat less bread doesn't mean you can't enjoy the flavors of your favorite sandwiches. It happens that the classic vegan tempeh reuben transforms effortlessly into a lovely meal in a bowl.

2 (8-ounce) packages tempeh,
   cut into ¼-inch-thick strips
¼ cup vegan mayonnaise
2 tablespoons ketchup
2 tablespoons sweet pickle relish

Salt and freshly ground black pepper
1 tablespoon olive oil
2 cups sauerkraut
4 slices vegan pumpernickel bread

Steam the tempeh in a double boiler over a saucepan of simmering water for 12 minutes. Set aside.

While the tempeh is steaming, combine the mayonnaise, ketchup, pickle relish, and salt and pepper to taste in a small bowl. Blend well and set aside.

Heat the oil in a large skillet over medium heat. Add the steamed tempeh and cook until golden brown, 5 to 7 minutes. Season with salt and pepper to taste. Add the sauerkraut, cover, and cook for 5 minutes, stirring occasionally to heat through.

Toast the bread and cut it diagonally into quarters. To serve, divide the tempeh and sauerkraut evenly into serving bowls and top with a spoonful of the reserved dressing. Stand 4 bread quarters around the edge of each bowl.

vegetable potpie bowls

serves 4

A toasted bread "lid" keeps these potpies quick and easy. If you prefer a pastry top instead of toast for your potpie, you can easily make four rounds out of a sheet of thawed vegan puff pastry or rolled-out pie dough. Just cut them out using a large cutter, or use a small bowl as a pattern and cut them out with a knife, then arrange on a baking sheet and bake in a preheated 425°F oven until golden brown, about 10 minutes.

1 (16-ounce) bag frozen mixed vegetables
1 tablespoon olive oil
1 medium yellow onion, finely chopped
2 tablespoons dry white wine
1½ cups home-cooked chickpeas, or
   1 (15.5-ounce) can, drained and rinsed
½ cup vegetable broth
2 tablespoons tahini

1 tablespoon white miso paste
1 tablespoon freshly
   squeezed lemon juice
½ teaspoon dried thyme
Salt and freshly ground black pepper
1 tablespoon minced fresh Italian parsley
4 slices bread (or other
   "lid"; see headnote)

Cook the frozen vegetables in a pot of boiling salted water until just tender, about 7 minutes. Drain and return to the pot. Set aside.

Heat the oil in a saucepan over medium heat. Add the onion, cover, and cook until softened, about 5 minutes. Scoop out all but about 2 tablespoons of the onion and add to the vegetables in the pot. To the remaining onion in the saucepan, stir in the wine, chickpeas, and broth and simmer over medium-high heat for 2 minutes to blend the flavors. Transfer the mixture to a blender or food processor. Add the tahini, miso, lemon juice, thyme, and salt and pepper to taste. Blend until smooth and creamy.

Stir the sauce into the vegetable mixture, add the parsley, and heat over low heat until hot, stirring frequently. Taste and adjust the seasonings, if needed.

While the vegetables are heating, toast the bread. Use a large cutter or a small bowl as a pattern to cut the toast into large rounds. To serve, spoon the vegetable mixture into serving bowls and top each with a toast "lid."

polenta with tuscan kale and cremini mushrooms

serves 4

For an even faster meal, use quick-cooking polenta and follow the directions on the package, or buy polenta that has already been cooked and warm it according to the package directions. Use regular kale and white mushrooms if Tuscan kale and cremini mushrooms are unavailable.

3 cups vegetable broth
1 cup yellow cornmeal
1 tablespoon olive oil
3 cloves garlic, minced
8 ounces cremini mushrooms, sliced
3 scallions, minced
8 ounces fresh Tuscan kale,
   coarsely chopped
1½ cups home-cooked cannellini or
   other white beans, or 1 (15.5-ounce)
   can, drained and rinsed

½ cup reconstituted or oil-packed
   sun-dried tomatoes, cut into strips
1 tablespoon freshly
   squeezed lemon juice
½ teaspoon dried thyme
Salt and freshly ground black pepper
2 tablespoons minced fresh
   basil or Italian parsley

Bring the broth to a boil in a large saucepan over high heat. (If the broth isn't very salty, add up to 1 teaspoon of salt.) When the water boils, add the cornmeal, stirring constantly with a wire whisk. Lower the heat to medium and cook, stirring frequently until thickened, 15 to 20 minutes.

Heat the oil in a saucepan over medium heat. Add the garlic, mushrooms, scallions, and kale and cook, stirring, for 6 to 8 minutes, until the vegetables are softened. Stir in the cannellini beans, tomatoes, lemon juice, and thyme. Season with salt and pepper to taste. Cook for another minute or two to heat through. Taste and adjust the seasonings, if needed. To serve, spoon the polenta into shallow serving bowls and then top with the vegetable mixture. Serve hot, sprinkled with the basil.

mediterranean tofu scram-bowls

serves 4

Sure, a tofu scramble makes a great breakfast, but I often rely on them for quick casual dinners, too. This is one of my favorite combos, filled with lots of veggies and Italian seasonings. Enjoy as is, or accompany these bowls with toasted Italian bread. Leftovers make a terrific wrap filling!

1 tablespoon olive oil or
   3 tablespoons water
1 small red onion, finely chopped
1 red bell pepper, seeded and chopped
8 ounces white mushrooms,
   thinly sliced or chopped
5 scallions, minced
1 pound firm tofu, well
   drained and crumbled
⅓ cup nutritional yeast
1 teaspoon garlic powder
1 teaspoon salt

½ teaspoon freshly ground black pepper
½ teaspoon dried marjoram
½ teaspoon dried basil
1 medium fresh tomato, chopped
2 cups chopped fresh spinach
¼ cup kalamata olives, pitted and halved
1 tablespoon capers (optional)
¼ cup vegetable broth or plain
   unsweetened almond milk
   or other nondairy milk
2 tablespoons chopped fresh
   basil or Italian parsley

Heat the oil in a large skillet over medium-high heat. Add the onion and bell pepper, cover, and cook until softened, about 4 minutes. Stir in the mushrooms and scallions and cook for 2 to 3 minutes longer. Add the tofu. Sprinkle the tofu with the nutritional yeast, garlic powder, salt, pepper, marjoram, and dried basil. Cook, stirring, for 3 to 4 minutes. Stir in the tomato, spinach, olives, and capers, if using.

If the mixture begins to stick, add a small amount of the broth, 1 tablespoon at a time. When the mixture is hot, divide it among serving bowls and sprinkle with the fresh basil.

manchurian chickpea bowls

serves 4

The flavor of Manchurian cauliflower is so intoxicatingly delicious that I decided to spread it around. It turns out that potatoes and chickpeas are perfect vehicles for the wondrous sauce that's made with ginger, garlic, tomato, and fragrant spices. Best of all, it's a meal in a bowl!

3 cups small cauliflower florets

1 large Yukon Gold potato, peeled
   and cut into 1-inch dice

1½ cups home-cooked chickpeas, or
   1 (15.5-ounce) can, drained and rinsed

1 cup frozen green peas, thawed

1 tablespoon olive oil or
   2 tablespoons water

1 large yellow onion, finely chopped

3 cloves garlic, minced

2 teaspoons finely grated fresh ginger

½ teaspoon ground coriander

¼ teaspoon ground cumin

¼ cup tomato paste

¼ cup ketchup

3 tablespoons tamari soy sauce

2 teaspoons hot sauce

2 teaspoons toasted sesame oil

1 cup water

Salt and freshly ground black pepper

2 scallions, minced

2 tablespoons chopped fresh cilantro

Steam the cauliflower and potato over boiling water until just tender. Remove from the heat and transfer to a large bowl. Add the chickpeas and green peas and set aside.

Heat the oil in a large deep skillet over medium heat. Add the onion, cover, and cook until softened, stirring occasionally, about 5 minutes. Add the garlic, ginger, coriander, and cumin and cook for 1 to 2 minutes. Stir in the tomato paste, ketchup, tamari, hot sauce, and sesame oil. Slowly stir in the water and simmer until the sauce is thickened and well blended, about 2 minutes. Taste and adjust the seasonings, if needed.

Add the chickpeas and vegetables to the skillet, stirring gently to coat with the sauce. Cook for 2 to 3 minutes to heat through. To serve, divide the mixture among serving bowls and sprinkle with the scallions and cilantro.

mexi-cali quinoa bowls
with pintos and corn

serves 4

These hearty quinoa bowls made with pinto beans, corn, and spinach are extremely versatile. I like to top them with avocado and hot sauce, but you can also spoon on some vegan sour cream, toasted pepitas, sliced pickled jalapeños, or sliced black olives. You can also substitute black beans for the pintos or use chard or kale instead of spinach.

1 tablespoon olive oil or ¼ cup water
1 large red onion, finely chopped
1 red bell pepper, seeded and chopped
3 cloves garlic, minced
1 teaspoon ground cumin
½ teaspoon smoked paprika
½ teaspoon dried marjoram
1 cup quinoa, well rinsed and drained
2 cups vegetable broth or water

Salt and freshly ground black pepper
2 cups frozen corn kernels
1 medium fresh tomato, chopped
2 scallions, minced
2 cups chopped fresh spinach
1½ cups home-cooked pinto beans, or
   1 (15.5-ounce) can, rinsed and drained
1 Hass avocado
Hot sauce, for serving

Heat the oil in a large saucepan over medium heat. Add the onion, bell pepper, and garlic and cook for 4 minutes to soften. Stir in the cumin, paprika, and marjoram, then add the quinoa, broth, and salt and pepper to taste, and bring to a boil. Lower the heat to a simmer, cover, and cook for 15 minutes.

Stir in the corn, tomato, scallions, spinach, and pinto beans and cook until the quinoa and vegetables are tender, about 10 minutes longer. Taste and adjust the seasonings, if needed.

To serve, halve and pit the avocado. Scoop out the flesh with a spoon and dice. Divide the mixture among serving bowls and top with the avocado. Serve with hot sauce as desired.

quinoa, white beans, and brussels sprouts with pecans and cranberries

serves 4

If you've never had roasted Brussels sprouts, you're in for a treat—their flavor becomes almost nutty when roasted. Combined with cooked quinoa, colorful cranberries, and crunchy pecans, they make a lovely bowl to enjoy on a cold winter night. Red quinoa looks especially lovely in this dish, although regular quinoa tastes just as good too.

8 ounces Brussels sprouts,
    trimmed and quartered
1 tablespoon olive oil
Salt and freshly ground black pepper
1 cup quinoa, well rinsed and drained
2 cups vegetable broth
1½ cups home-cooked white beans, or
    1 (15.5-ounce) can, drained and rinsed

3 scallions, chopped
1 tablespoon freshly
    squeezed lemon juice
1 teaspoon minced fresh thyme
    or ½ teaspoon dried
½ cup toasted pecan pieces
½ cup dried cranberries

Preheat the oven to 425°F and lightly oil a baking sheet. Spread the Brussels sprouts on the baking sheet. Drizzle with the olive oil and season with salt and pepper. Roast until tender, about 10 minutes.

While the sprouts are roasting, combine the quinoa and broth in a saucepan and bring to a boil. Add salt to taste, lower the heat to a simmer, cover, and cook until the quinoa is just tender, about 18 minutes.

Stir in the beans, scallions, lemon juice, and thyme. To serve, combine the quinoa and Brussels sprouts in a serving bowl. Add the pecans and cranberries and toss gently to combine. Serve hot.

stir-fries, sautés, and skillet dishes

Whether you use a skillet, wok, or sauté pan, stovetop cooking can really be a flash in the pan, especially when you have cooked grains and beans on hand. Using a variety of fresh vegetables helps ensure that these recipes are as nutritious as they are quick and easy.

From Asian stir-fries such as General Tso's Tofu (page 72) and Sesame-Orange Tempeh with Snow Peas (page 77) to home-style skillet dishes including Unstuffed Cabbage (page 76) and Quinoa-Roni Pilaf (page 89), these versatile recipes will help you get a wholesome and delicious meal on the table in minutes.

eggplant and chickpeas puttanesca

serves 4

The bold flavors of puttanesca sauce, heady with garlic, olives, and capers, match well with chickpeas and eggplant. This new take on the classic pasta sauce can be enjoyed on its own, although it is quite wonderful served over polenta or, of course, pasta. It's also great as a crostini topping or tossed with spaghetti squash. If you're not a fan of eggplant, you can still make this luscious recipe by substituting zucchini or mushrooms for the eggplant.

1 tablespoon olive oil
5 cloves garlic, minced
1 medium eggplant, peeled
   and cut into ½-inch dice
1 (14.5-ounce) can diced
   tomatoes, including juices
2 tablespoons tomato paste
½ teaspoon dried basil
½ teaspoon dried oregano
¼ teaspoon red pepper flakes

1½ cups home-cooked chickpeas, or
   1 (15.5-ounce) can, drained and rinsed
Salt and freshly ground black pepper
¼ cup kalamata olives, pitted and halved
¼ cup sliced green olives
1 tablespoon capers
¼ cup chopped fresh basil leaves
2 tablespoons minced fresh
   Italian parsley

Heat the oil in a large saucepan over medium heat. Add the garlic and cook until fragrant, 1 minute. Stir in the eggplant, diced tomatoes, tomato paste, dried basil, oregano, and red pepper flakes. Stir in a little water if the mixture is too dry. Add the chickpeas and season with salt and pepper to taste. Cover and cook until the eggplant is tender, about 15 minutes. Stir in the olives, capers, basil, and parsley. Serve hot.

general tso's tofu

serves 4

Now you can enjoy the flavors of this Chinese take-out favorite at home and, best of all, make it with tofu instead of chicken. To complete the meal, serve with fresh cooked rice and steamed broccoli.

½ cup plus 1 tablespoon cornstarch
14 to 16 ounces extra-firm tofu,
    drained and cut into 1-inch dice
Neutral vegetable oil, for frying
3 scallions, chopped
1 tablespoon grated fresh ginger
2 cloves garlic, minced

1 cup vegetable broth
3 tablespoons tamari soy sauce
¼ cup natural sugar
½ teaspoon red pepper flakes
1 tablespoon sherry
1 tablespoon rice vinegar
¼ cup water

Place the ½ cup cornstarch in a shallow bowl. Add the tofu and toss to coat completely.

Heat a thin layer of oil in a large skillet. Add the tofu and cook until golden, turning as needed. Remove from the pan and set aside. Return the skillet to the heat. Add the scallions, ginger, and garlic and stir-fry for 1 minute. Stir in the broth, tamari, sugar, red pepper flakes, sherry, and vinegar. Mix the water with the remaining 1 tablespoon cornstarch and pour into the mixture, stirring well. Add the reserved tofu and spoon the sauce over the tofu to coat evenly. Serve hot.

fiery korean stir-fry

serves 4

This spicy stir-fry made with tofu and napa cabbage can be enjoyed alone, served over rice, or tossed with cooked noodles. Seasoned with ginger, tamari, and sesame oil, it gets its heat from a combination of cayenne and red pepper flakes, but if you have some gochujang, a spicy Korean chili paste, or another favorite Asian chili paste, you can use it instead of the red pepper flakes and cayenne.

1 tablespoon neutral vegetable oil
14 to 16 ounces extra-firm tofu,
    drained and cut into ½-inch dice
1 tablespoon sesame seeds
1 medium napa cabbage (about
    1½ pounds), cut into strips
3 cloves garlic, minced
2 carrots, coarsely shredded
5 scallions, chopped

1 teaspoon grated fresh ginger
3 tablespoons tamari soy sauce
3 tablespoons water
2 tablespoons rice vinegar
2 teaspoons natural sugar
1 tablespoon toasted sesame oil
¼ teaspoon red pepper flakes
¼ teaspoon salt
¼ teaspoon cayenne

Heat the oil in a large nonstick skillet or wok over medium-high heat. Add the tofu and stir-fry until lightly browned. Add the sesame seeds and continue to stir-fry for 1 minute, then remove the tofu and sesame seeds from the skillet and reserve.

In the same skillet, over medium heat, add the cabbage, garlic, carrots, scallions, and ginger and stir-fry for 3 minutes to soften. Stir in the tamari, water, vinegar, sugar, sesame oil, red pepper flakes, salt, and cayenne. Stir-fry for about 5 minutes, or until the vegetables are crisp-tender. Return the tofu and sesame seeds to the skillet and continue to stir-fry to heat through. Serve hot.

tofu and green beans
with hoisin-almond sauce

serves 4

This dish is super-versatile: You can substitute broccoli or asparagus for the green beans, use tempeh or seitan instead of tofu, and make it more or less spicy according to your taste. Serve as is, or for a heartier meal, spoon it over cooked rice or quinoa or toss it with cooked rice noodles.

12 ounces green beans, trimmed
    and cut into 1-inch pieces
1 tablespoon neutral vegetable oil
1 pound extra-firm tofu, cut
    into ½-inch dice
3 scallions, minced
2 cloves garlic, minced
1 teaspoon grated fresh ginger
½ teaspoon hot red pepper flakes
Salt and freshly ground black pepper

1 tablespoon cornstarch
2 tablespoons tamari soy sauce
2 tablespoons hoisin sauce
2 tablespoons almond butter
2 tablespoons rice vinegar
2 teaspoons agave nectar
    or pure maple syrup
1 teaspoon toasted sesame oil
¾ cup vegetable broth
2 tablespoons chopped peanuts

Steam the green beans until just tender, about 5 minutes, then rinse under cold water to stop the cooking process. Set aside.

Heat the vegetable oil in a large skillet over medium-high heat. Add the tofu and cook until golden brown all over, about 8 minutes. Add the scallions, garlic, ginger, and red pepper flakes. Season with salt and pepper to taste.

In a small bowl, combine the cornstarch and tamari, stirring to dissolve the cornstarch. Stir in the hoisin sauce, almond butter, rice vinegar, agave, and sesame oil, stirring to blend. Stir in the broth until smooth.

Stir the sauce and the reserved green beans into the tofu mixture and cook for a few minutes, stirring, to heat through and thicken the sauce. Serve hot, sprinkled with the peanuts.

moroccan bistilla pilaf

serves 4 to 6

A bistilla or bisteeya is actually a pastry-wrapped dish that can be fairly time-consuming to prepare. This recipe gives you all the flavor of a tasty bistilla without all the work—despite a long ingredients list, the dish comes together in a snap. If you crave that flaky pastry, you can bake a few puff pastry squares or rounds to top each serving.

1 tablespoon olive oil
1 medium yellow onion, chopped
2 carrots, thinly sliced
2 cloves garlic, minced
1 medium zucchini, chopped
2 teaspoons grated fresh ginger
1 teaspoon ground coriander
½ teaspoon ground cumin
¼ teaspoon ground cinnamon
¼ teaspoon cayenne
¾ cup couscous
1¼ cups vegetable broth

1½ cups home-cooked chickpeas, or
    1 (15.5-ounce) can, drained and rinsed
½ cup frozen green peas, thawed
½ cup chopped dried apricots
⅓ cup raisins
1 tablespoon freshly
    squeezed lemon juice
2 teaspoons finely grated lemon zest
Salt and freshly ground black pepper
¼ cup chopped fresh cilantro
    or Italian parsley
⅓ cup toasted slivered almonds

Heat the oil in a large deep skillet or saucepan over medium heat. Add the onion and carrots, cover, and cook until softened, about 5 minutes. Stir in the garlic, zucchini, and ginger and cook for 2 minutes. Stir in the coriander, cumin, cinnamon, and cayenne. Then stir in the couscous, followed by the broth. Bring to a boil, then stir in the chickpeas, green peas, apricots, raisins, lemon juice, and zest.

Remove from the heat, season with salt and pepper to taste, cover, and set aside for 5 minutes. To serve, fluff with a fork and transfer to a serving bowl. Top with the cilantro and almonds.

unstuffed cabbage

serves 4

Stuffed cabbage rolls are one of those comfort food dishes I crave during the winter months, but I don't always have time to make them. For those times when I want the flavor of stuffed cabbage rolls without the lengthy prep time, I combine all the ingredients in a skillet for a delicious stir-fry.

2 tablespoons olive oil
1 large yellow onion, minced
6 cups coarsely chopped green cabbage
2 cloves garlic, minced
8 ounces cremini mushrooms, chopped
1½ cups your choice of reconstituted TVP granules, crumbled extra-firm tofu, chopped seitan, or chopped steamed tempeh

1 teaspoon dried thyme
2 cups cooked brown rice
2 tablespoons tomato paste
2 tablespoons tamari soy sauce
1 tablespoon natural sugar
1 tablespoon cider vinegar
Salt and freshly ground black pepper

Heat the oil in a large nonstick skillet over medium-high heat. Add the onion, cabbage, and garlic and stir-fry for 5 minutes to soften. Add the mushrooms, your choice of protein, thyme, and cooked rice. Stir-fry for 5 minutes longer.

In a small bowl, blend together the tomato paste, tamari, sugar, and vinegar, then stir into the skillet, stir-frying to blend the flavors. Season with salt and pepper to taste. Cook for a few minutes longer, until the vegetables are soft and the flavors are well blended.

sesame-orange tempeh with snow peas

serves 4

The bright and bold flavors of ginger, orange, sesame oil, rice vinegar, and tamari are a good match for the tempeh. Paired with carrots and snow peas, it makes a lovely dish that is delicious served over cooked rice or quinoa. Instead of snow peas, you can substitute another vegetable, such as broccoli or asparagus. If you're not a fan of tempeh, try this with seitan, soy curls, or extra-firm tofu.

8 ounces tempeh, cut into 1-inch pieces
2 tablespoons cornstarch
3 tablespoons tamari soy sauce
3 tablespoons agave nectar
1 tablespoon toasted sesame oil
3 tablespoons rice vinegar
½ cup freshly squeezed orange juice

1 tablespoon neutral vegetable
    oil or ¼ cup water
2 carrots, thinly sliced diagonally
3 to 4 ounces snow peas, trimmed
2 teaspoons grated fresh ginger
Finely grated zest of 1 orange
2 tablespoons water
2 tablespoons black sesame seeds

Steam the tempeh for 15 minutes in a steamer over boiling water. While the tempeh is steaming, combine the cornstarch, tamari, agave, sesame oil, vinegar, and orange juice in a small bowl, stirring to mix.

Heat the oil in a large skillet or wok over medium-high heat. Add the tempeh and carrots and stir-fry for 2 minutes. Add the snow peas and ginger and stir-fry for 2 minutes longer. Stir in the orange zest and the 2 tablespoons water, then stir in the reserved sauce mixture. Add the sesame seeds and cook for another minute or two, stirring to coat the tempeh and vegetables with the sauce and to allow the sauce to thicken a bit. Serve hot.

succotash fritters

serves 4

I'm a sucker for succotash, especially in the summer, when fresh corn and lima beans are plentiful. In the winter, I use frozen corn and limas. The first time I made these fritters, it was a way to use up leftover succotash, but they're good enough not to wait for leftovers.

1½ cups lima beans
1½ cups corn kernels
½ cup old-fashioned rolled oats
½ cup minced yellow onion
¼ cup chopped fresh parsley
   (either curly or Italian)
¾ to 1 teaspoon salt

¼ teaspoon freshly ground black pepper
2 tablespoons jarred chopped pimientos
   or roasted red bell peppers, blotted dry
3 scallions, minced
¼ cup medium-grind yellow cornmeal,
   plus more for dredging
Olive oil, for frying

Cook the lima beans in a saucepan of boiling water until tender, about 7 minutes. About 1 minute before the beans are cooked, stir the corn kernels into the beans and continue cooking for the final minute. Drain well, blot dry, and set aside.

In a food processor, process the oats to a powder. Add the onion, parsley, and about 2 cups of the lima and corn mixture. Season with the salt and pepper and process until smooth. Scrape the mixture into a bowl and fold in the pimientos, the remaining 1 cup of limas and corn kernels, the scallions, and the ¼ cup cornmeal. Mix well. Shape the mixture into patties 3 to 4 inches in diameter and about ⅓ inch thick. If the mixture is too sticky, add additional cornmeal, a tablespoon or two at a time, until you can shape it into patties. Dredge the patties on both sides with cornmeal.

Heat a thin layer of oil in a large nonstick skillet over medium heat. Add the fritters and cook until golden brown on both sides, turning once, about 4 minutes per side. Serve hot.

spicy ginger-lime portobellos and broccoli

serves 4

To increase the protein in this delicious stir-fry, add 8 ounces of extra-firm tofu, seitan, or steamed tempeh strips when you add the mushrooms. For a spicy variation, add 1 teaspoon of Asian chili paste to the sauce mixture. Enjoy alone or served over hot cooked rice or quinoa.

1 tablespoon neutral vegetable oil

1 medium yellow onion, halved
   and thinly sliced

3 cups small broccoli florets

4 large portobello mushroom
   caps, cut into ¼-inch strips

1 tablespoon grated fresh ginger

1 teaspoon minced garlic

2 tablespoons tamari soy sauce

3 tablespoons freshly squeezed lime juice

1 tablespoon agave nectar
   or natural sugar

1 teaspoon Asian chili paste or
   ½ teaspoon red pepper flakes

2 teaspoons cornstarch

¼ cup water

Heat the oil in a large skillet or wok over medium-high heat. Add the onion and broccoli and stir-fry for 4 to 5 minutes, then add the mushrooms and continue to stir-fry for 2 minutes longer. Stir in the ginger and garlic.

In a small bowl, combine the tamari, lime juice, agave, and chili paste, stirring to combine. Stir in the cornstarch, then stir in the water. Pour the mixture into the skillet and cook, stirring, until the sauce thickens, 2 to 3 minutes longer. Serve hot.

tempeh with artichokes and olives

serves 4

This hearty dish is great served as is with some crusty bread and a salad or over cooked pasta, rice, or quinoa. If you're not a fan of tempeh, you can substitute seitan, extra-firm tofu, or cooked chickpeas.

1 pound tempeh, cut into ½-inch dice
1 tablespoon olive oil
1 red bell pepper, seeded and chopped
5 cloves garlic, minced
3 scallions, minced
¼ cup dry white wine or vegetable broth
1 (14-ounce) can artichoke hearts, drained and coarsely chopped

½ cup reconstituted or oil-packed sun-dried tomatoes, cut into thin strips
½ teaspoon red pepper flakes
Salt and freshly ground black pepper
½ cup kalamata olives, pitted and halved
2 tablespoons minced fresh basil or Italian parsley

Steam the tempeh for 15 minutes in a steamer over boiling water. While the tempeh is steaming, heat the oil in a skillet over medium heat. Add the bell pepper and garlic and cook until softened, about 2 minutes. Add the tempeh and cook until lightly browned. Stir in the scallions, then add the wine and cook for 1 minute longer. Add the artichokes, tomatoes, and red pepper flakes. Season to taste with salt and pepper.

Cook, stirring occasionally, until the vegetables are softened and the flavors are well blended. If the mixture is too dry, add a little water. Stir in the olives and basil and serve hot.

vegetable fried rice and quinoa

serves 4

Take-out fried rice is a perennial favorite, but it can be loaded with oil and there's never enough vegetables—it's mostly rice. This recipe keeps the oil to a minimum while still retaining the flavor. Best of all, you can have it your way: Add as few or as many vegetables as you like, and even use quinoa for all or part of the rice. Use this recipe as a guide to customize your own version, using whatever cold grains you have on hand or vegetables you need to use up. You can also leave out the tofu and substitute crumbled steamed tempeh, chopped seitan, or cooked shelled edamame.

1 cup pressed and crumbled
   extra-firm tofu
2 tablespoons tamari soy sauce
2 teaspoons toasted sesame oil
Salt and freshly ground black pepper
1 tablespoon neutral vegetable oil
1 large yellow onion, chopped
2 cloves garlic, minced

1 carrot, coarsely shredded
1 small red bell pepper,
   seeded and chopped
2 cups chopped bok choy
1¾ cups cold cooked rice
1¾ cups cold cooked quinoa
   (or additional rice)
½ cup frozen green peas, thawed

In a bowl, combine the crumbled tofu with 1 tablespoon of the tamari and 1 teaspoon of the sesame oil. Season with salt and pepper to taste and mix well. Set aside.

Heat the vegetable oil in a large skillet or wok over medium-high heat. Add the onion, garlic, and carrot and stir-fry for 30 seconds. Add the bell pepper and bok choy. Lower the heat to medium and stir-fry for 3 to 4 minutes to soften the vegetables.

Add the rice, quinoa, peas, the remaining 1 tablespoon tamari, the remaining 1 teaspoon sesame oil, and salt and pepper to taste. Increase the heat to medium-high and stir-fry for 2 minutes more. Stir in the reserved tofu mixture and stir-fry for 2 to 3 minutes longer to heat through. Taste and adjust the seasonings, if needed. Serve hot.

chickpeas niçoise

serves 4

Elements of the classic Niçoise salad join forces with tasty chickpeas in this savory sauté. It's a delicious one-dish meal on its own, but I can't help serving it with some toasted French bread.

1 pound small red potatoes,
   quartered or sliced ¼ inch thick
6 ounces green beans, trimmed
   and cut into 2-inch pieces
2 tablespoons olive oil
3 cloves garlic, minced
3 scallions, minced
Salt and freshly ground black pepper

1½ cups home-cooked chickpeas, or
   1 (15.5-ounce) can, drained and rinsed
1 cup cherry tomatoes, halved
2 tablespoons kalamata or Niçoise
   olives, pitted and halved
1 tablespoon white wine vinegar
2 tablespoons minced fresh
   Italian parsley
2 tablespoons minced fresh basil

Steam the potatoes for 5 minutes in a steamer over boiling water, then add the green beans and steam until both are just tender, about 5 minutes longer. Run the vegetables under cold water to stop the cooking process, and set aside.

Heat the oil in a large skillet over medium heat. Add the garlic and scallions and cook until fragrant, 30 seconds. Add the potatoes and green beans, season with salt and pepper to taste, and sauté for 2 minutes. Add the chickpeas, tomatoes, and olives and heat through, about 2 minutes longer. Drizzle on the vinegar and add the parsley and basil. Toss gently to combine and serve.

black beans and spinach with tomato-avocado salsa

serves 4

This easy and versatile dish can be enjoyed as is, served over rice, wrapped in a tortilla, scooped up with chips, or spooned into a baked tortilla bowl. If you want to add some spices, stir in some ground chili powder and cumin when you add the beans.

1 tablespoon olive oil
1 large red onion, minced
2 cloves garlic, minced
3 cups home-cooked black beans, or
  2 (15.5-ounce) cans, drained and rinsed
8 ounces fresh baby spinach,
  coarsely chopped
Salt and freshly ground black pepper

1½ cups cherry or grape tomatoes,
  halved or quartered
2 scallions, minced
1 small fresh hot chile, seeded
  and minced (optional)
1 tablespoon freshly squeezed lime juice
1 Hass avocado
2 tablespoons chopped fresh cilantro

Heat the oil in a skillet over medium heat. Add the onion and garlic, cover, and cook until softened, about 5 minutes. Add the black beans and spinach, stirring to wilt the spinach. Season with salt and pepper to taste, then decrease the heat to low, cover, and cook for a few minutes longer while you make the salsa.

In a bowl, combine the tomatoes, scallions, chile, if using, and lime juice. Halve and pit the avocado. Scoop out the flesh with a spoon and chop. Add the avocado, cilantro, and salt and pepper to taste to the salsa. Toss gently to combine. Serve the bean mixture topped with the salsa.

figgy quinoa pilaf

serves 4

I love the combination of textures and flavors in this colorful pilaf. For a more substantial meal, you can stir in cooked chickpeas when you add the figs. This dish can also be made with rice, but it will take longer to cook.

2 teaspoons olive oil or
  3 tablespoons water
2 cloves garlic, minced
2 teaspoons grated fresh ginger
1 large carrot, coarsely shredded
1 cup quinoa, well rinsed and drained
2 cups water or vegetable broth

Salt and freshly ground black pepper
½ cup dried figs, stemmed and
  chopped or quartered
2 scallions, minced
3 tablespoons shelled roasted
  pistachios (optional)

Heat the oil in a saucepan over medium heat. Add the garlic and ginger and cook until fragrant, about 30 seconds. Stir in the carrot, then add the quinoa and the 2 cups water. Salt the water, cover, and bring to a boil. Lower the heat to a simmer and cook, covered, for 15 minutes. A few minutes before the quinoa is tender, season with black pepper and stir in the figs, scallions, and pistachios, if using. Continue to cook until the quinoa is tender and all the liquid is evaporated, about 5 minutes longer. Taste and adjust the seasonings, if needed. Serve hot.

lemon pesto zucchini and white beans

serves 4

The flavors of lemon and almonds punctuate this refreshing pesto that transforms simple white beans and zucchini into a special dish. As is, it makes a great side dish, but you can turn it into a main dish by serving it over cooked pasta or your favorite cooked grain.

3 tablespoons olive oil
4 small zucchini, trimmed
    and thinly sliced
3 scallions, chopped
Salt and freshly ground black pepper
1½ cups home-cooked white beans, or
    1 (15.5-ounce) can, drained and rinsed

3 cloves garlic, crushed
2 teaspoons finely grated lemon zest
⅓ cup almonds or pine nuts
1 cup packed fresh basil leaves
1 tablespoon freshly
    squeezed lemon juice

Heat 1 tablespoon of the oil in a large nonstick skillet over medium heat. Add the zucchini and scallions and stir-fry until softened, 5 to 7 minutes. Season with salt and pepper to taste, and stir in the white beans. Keep warm.

While the zucchini is cooking, combine the garlic, lemon zest, and almonds in a blender or food processor and mince to a paste. Add the basil, lemon juice, salt and pepper to taste, and the remaining 2 tablespoons olive oil and process to a paste. If the mixture is too dry, add a little water to achieve the desired consistency.

Add the pesto to the pan with the zucchini and beans and stir gently to combine and heat through. Taste and adjust the seasonings, if needed. Serve hot.

sukiyaki shiitakes and tofu

serves 4

At once light and satisfying, this delicious dish combines tofu and chewy shiitakes with fresh spinach and crunchy bean sprouts in a delectable sauce made fragrant with sake or sherry. Served over freshly cooked brown rice, it makes an easy and elegant meal.

1 tablespoon neutral vegetable oil
1 large yellow onion, halved
   and thinly sliced
8 ounces shiitake mushroom
   caps, cut into strips
1 pound extra-firm tofu, drained
   and cut into 1-inch dice
2 tablespoons tamari soy sauce
¼ cup sake or dry sherry
1 teaspoon natural sugar

¼ teaspoon freshly ground black pepper
1½ cups vegetable broth
8 ounces fresh spinach, stemmed
   and cut into strips
1½ cups fresh bean sprouts (4 ounces)
1½ tablespoons cornstarch dissolved
   in 2 tablespoons water
⅓ cup fresh Thai basil leaves (optional)
Cooked brown rice, for serving

Heat the oil in a large skillet over medium-high heat. Add the onion and mushrooms and stir-fry until softened, about 5 minutes. Stir in the tofu, tamari, sake, sugar, pepper, and broth and bring to a boil. Add the spinach and bean sprouts and cook until the spinach is wilted, about 1 minute. Stir in the cornstarch mixture and cook, stirring, until slightly thickened. Taste and adjust the seasonings, if needed. Stir in the Thai basil, if using. Serve hot over rice.

spicy ginger tempeh and bok choy

serves 4

If you're a tempeh fan, you'll love the way it absorbs the flavorful sauce in this quick and easy stir-fry. This is best served over rice or quinoa and is a good reason to keep cooked grains on hand so that you can enjoy your meal in just minutes.

1 pound tempeh, cut into ½-inch dice
1 tablespoon neutral vegetable oil
1 medium yellow onion,
   chopped or thinly sliced
6 cups coarsely chopped bok choy
Salt and freshly ground black pepper
½ red bell pepper, seeded and chopped
½ cup chopped mushrooms (any variety)
4 scallions, chopped
3 cloves garlic, minced

2 tablespoons grated fresh ginger
2 tablespoons tamari soy sauce
1 tablespoon rice vinegar
1 tablespoon black bean paste
1 teaspoon Asian chili paste
1 teaspoon natural sugar
1½ cups water
1 tablespoon cornstarch dissolved
   in 2 tablespoons water

Steam the tempeh in a steamer over boiling water for 15 minutes. Set aside.

Heat the oil in a large skillet or wok over medium-high heat. Add the onion and bok choy and stir-fry until wilted. Season with salt and pepper to taste and remove from the skillet.

In the same skillet over medium heat, add the tempeh and stir-fry until browned, about 4 minutes. Add the bell pepper, mushrooms, scallions, garlic, and ginger and stir-fry for 1 minute to soften. Stir in the tamari, vinegar, bean paste, chili paste, sugar, and water and bring to a boil. Lower the heat to a simmer and cook for 5 minutes. Stir in the cornstarch mixture and cook for 5 minutes longer, stirring to thicken. Stir in the reserved greens and cook for 1 minute longer to heat through. Serve hot.

quinoa-roni pilaf

serves 4

Inspired by the "San Francisco treat," this tasty pilaf is much healthier than the original. Feel free to add additional veggies, such as shredded carrot, chopped spinach, or frozen peas. Or you can chop any cooked leftover vegetable you may have on hand and add it during the last few minutes.

1 tablespoon olive oil or ¼ cup water
1 medium yellow onion, minced
3 cloves garlic, minced
¾ cup quinoa, well rinsed and drained
2 cups vegetable broth
1 teaspoon dried basil or marjoram
3 ounces spaghetti, broken
   into 1-inch pieces

1½ cups home-cooked white beans, or
   1 (15.5-ounce) can, drained and rinsed
2 tablespoons chopped reconstituted
   or oil-packed sun-dried tomatoes
¼ cup chopped fresh Italian parsley
Salt and freshly ground black pepper

Heat the oil in a large saucepan over medium heat. Add the onion, cover, and cook for 4 minutes to soften. Stir in the garlic and cook for 1 minute longer, then stir in the quinoa, broth, and basil and bring to a boil. Lower the heat to a simmer and cook, covered, for 7 minutes.

Stir in the spaghetti, beans, and tomatoes. Cover and cook until the quinoa and spaghetti are tender, 12 to 15 minutes longer.

Stir in the parsley and season with salt and pepper to taste. Serve hot.

quinoa with fennel and black olives

serves 4

Think of this pilaf when fresh fennel and tomatoes are in season. Although the slightly licorice flavor of fennel fades into the background when cooked, I still like to complement it with a similarly fragrant herb such as basil or tarragon.

1¾ cups vegetable broth
1 fennel bulb, trimmed and
   either chopped or halved
   lengthwise and thinly sliced
1 cup quinoa, well rinsed and drained
5 scallions, chopped
1½ cups home-cooked white beans, or
   1 (15.5-ounce) can, drained and rinsed

Salt and freshly ground black pepper
2 medium fresh tomatoes (about
   12 ounces), chopped, or 1 (14.5-ounce)
   can diced tomatoes, drained
¼ cup kalamata olives,
   pitted and chopped
¼ cup chopped fresh basil
2 teaspoons freshly squeezed lemon juice

Bring the broth to a boil in a large saucepan. Add the fennel and quinoa and return to a boil, then lower the heat to medium. Stir in the scallions, beans, and salt and pepper to taste. Cover and cook for 15 minutes or until the quinoa is just tender.

Stir in the tomatoes, olives, basil, and lemon juice. Taste and adjust the seasonings, if needed. Serve hot.

bulgur pilaf with chickpeas and cranberries

serves 4

I love the way the sweet cranberries and crunchy walnuts play against the creamy chickpeas and nutty bulgur. This hearty pilaf is equally delicious served hot, cold, or at room temperature.

2 cups water or vegetable broth
1 cup medium-grind bulgur
3 scallions, minced
Salt and freshly ground black pepper
1½ cups home-cooked chickpeas, or
   1 (15.5-ounce) can, drained and rinsed

½ cup dried cranberries
½ cup chopped toasted walnut pieces
2 tablespoons chopped fresh
   Italian parsley or mint

Bring the water to a boil in a large saucepan. Add the bulgur and scallions and stir to combine. Decrease the heat to low and season with salt and pepper to taste. Cover and simmer until the bulgur is tender and the liquid is absorbed, about 8 minutes.

Remove the pan from the heat and stir in the chickpeas, cranberries, and walnuts. Cover and let stand for 10 minutes. Stir in the parsley and serve.

black beans and bulgur
with carrots and figs

serves 4

Sweet figs and crunchy carrots highlight this satisfying pilaf made with bulgur and black beans. This is one of those stick-to-your-ribs dishes that has the flavors and textures of a complex recipe yet comes together in minutes.

½ cup medium-grind bulgur
1¼ cups hot vegetable broth
1 tablespoon olive oil or ¼ cup water
1 medium yellow onion, finely chopped
1 teaspoon dried thyme or marjoram
2 to 3 medium carrots, coarsely shredded
3 scallions, chopped

1½ cups home-cooked black beans, or
   1 (15.5-ounce) can, drained and rinsed
1 cup chopped fresh or dried figs
2 tablespoons freshly
   squeezed lemon juice
Salt and freshly ground black pepper

Place the bulgur in a bowl. Add the hot broth and set aside for 15 minutes.

Heat the oil in a large skillet over medium heat. Add the onion and cook until softened, about 5 minutes. Add the thyme, carrots, scallions, black beans, and the soaked bulgur. Decrease the heat to low, cover, and simmer until the ingredients are tender and the flavors are well blended, about 10 minutes.

Stir in the figs and lemon juice and season with salt and pepper to taste. Taste and adjust the seasonings, if needed. Serve hot.

pineapple-curry tempeh

serves 4

The pineapple-curry yogurt sauce is so good that you'll want to eat it with a spoon, but save some for the fragrant spice-rubbed tempeh. Serve over cooked rice or quinoa with your favorite vegetables.

1 pound tempeh, cut into ½-inch dice
¾ cup coconut vegan yogurt
¾ cup canned crushed pineapple
1¾ teaspoons curry powder
1 tablespoon tamari soy sauce
½ teaspoon ground coriander

½ teaspoon ground cumin
Salt and freshly ground black pepper
1 tablespoon neutral vegetable oil
4 scallions, chopped
2 tablespoons chopped
   fresh cilantro or mint

Steam the tempeh in a steamer over boiling water for 15 minutes.

While the tempeh is steaming, combine the yogurt, pineapple, and ¾ teaspoon of the curry powder in a small bowl; set aside.

Transfer the steamed tempeh to a medium bowl and add the tamari, the remaining 1 teaspoon curry powder, the coriander, cumin, and salt and pepper to taste. Toss to coat the tempeh with the spice mixture.

Heat the oil in a medium nonstick skillet over medium-high heat. Add the tempeh and scallions and stir-fry until nicely browned, about 5 minutes. Serve the tempeh topped with the yogurt mixture and sprinkled with the cilantro.

big bang tofu

serves 4

Made with only three ingredients, the quick and easy sauce here provides a big bang of flavor tossed with the lightly fried tofu. When making the sauce, add the sriracha a little at a time to be sure it turns out at the heat level you prefer.

⅓ cup Asian sweet chili sauce
⅓ cup vegan mayonnaise
1 to 2 tablespoons sriracha sauce
14 to 16 ounces extra-firm tofu,
   drained and pressed

2 tablespoons cornstarch
Salt and freshly ground black pepper
1 tablespoon neutral vegetable oil

In a small bowl, combine the chili sauce, mayonnaise, and sriracha and mix until thoroughly blended. Set aside.

Cut the tofu into ½-inch dice and place in a bowl. Sprinkle with the cornstarch and salt and pepper to taste and toss to coat the tofu.

Heat the oil in a large nonstick skillet over medium-high heat. Add the tofu and stir-fry until golden brown, about 7 minutes. To serve, toss the tofu with the reserved sauce and serve hot.

black bean and sweet potato picadillo

serves 4

Inspired by the popular Latin American dish, this version is made with black beans instead of meat and features sweet potatoes rather than white potatoes. Serve over cooked rice or quinoa.

1 tablespoon neutral vegetable oil
   or ¼ cup water
1 medium yellow onion, finely chopped
1 small red bell pepper,
   seeded and chopped
2 cloves garlic, minced
1 teaspoon ground cumin
1 teaspoon dried oregano
2 tablespoons tomato paste

½ cup vegetable broth
1 sweet potato, peeled and
   coarsely shredded
1½ cups home-cooked black beans, or
   1 (15.5-ounce) can, drained and rinsed
⅓ cup raisins
⅓ cup small pimiento-stuffed green olives
Salt and freshly ground black pepper

Heat the oil in a large skillet over medium-high heat. Add the onion, bell pepper, and garlic and cook for 5 minutes to soften. Stir in the cumin, oregano, tomato paste, broth, and sweet potato. Lower the heat to medium. Cover and cook for about 10 minutes, or until the vegetables are tender. Stir in the black beans, raisins, olives, and salt and pepper to taste. Cook uncovered for about 5 more minutes to heat through and blend the flavors. Serve hot.

chai-spiced rice and chickpeas

serves 4

If you're a fan of chai, you'll love what it does for rice. This fragrant and flavorful dish features chickpeas and carrots, but you can substitute other beans or vegetables, if you prefer. The final flourish of almonds, raisins, and fresh parsley brings it all together.

2¼ cups water
2 spiced chai tea bags
1 cup brown basmati rice, soaked
    and drained (see Note)
½ teaspoon salt
1½ cups home-cooked chickpeas, or
    1 (15.5-ounce) can, drained and rinsed

3 scallions, minced
1 medium carrot, coarsely shredded
3 tablespoons toasted slivered almonds
3 tablespoons golden raisins
    or dried cranberries
2 tablespoons chopped fresh Italian
    parsley, mint, or cilantro

Bring the water to a boil in a covered saucepan. Add the tea bags, rice, and salt and return to a boil, then lower the heat to a simmer, cover, and continue to cook until the water is absorbed and the rice is tender, about 30 minutes.

Remove the tea bags. Stir in the chickpeas, scallions, carrot, almonds, raisins, and parsley. Serve hot.

note: Most everyone knows that short-grain brown rice takes longer to cook than long-grain brown rice. But what many people don't realize is that even for the same type of rice—for instance, brown basmati—the rice may take anywhere from 25 to 45 minutes to cook. If you know your brand of rice takes longer to cook, you can shorten the cooking time by soaking your rice in hot water for about an hour before cooking (or you can soak it in warm or cold water for several hours or overnight in the refrigerator). Then just drain and it will be ready to use in your recipe. If you want to get dinner on the table faster, other options to try include using quick-cooking "instant" brown rice or switching to a quicker-cooking grain, such as quinoa.

pan-seared portobellos
with white beans and spinach

serves 4

Getting a nice sear on thick slices of meaty portobellos makes this a lovely and elegant dish. It almost tastes too good to be this quick and easy! To complete the meal, serve over rice, quinoa, or pasta. For a creamy, stroganoff-like variation, puree the beans in a food processor before adding to the mushroom mixture.

1 tablespoon olive oil
4 portobello mushroom caps,
    cut into ½-inch slices
2 shallots, minced
3 cloves garlic, minced
1 teaspoon minced fresh oregano
    or ½ teaspoon dried
2 teaspoons minced fresh basil
    or ½ teaspoon dried
½ cup dry white wine or sherry

1 tablespoon freshly
    squeezed lemon juice
1 tablespoon minced fresh Italian parsley
½ teaspoon salt
¼ teaspoon freshly ground black pepper
8 ounces fresh baby spinach,
    coarsely chopped
1½ cups home-cooked cannellini
    beans, or 1 (15.5-ounce) can,
    drained and rinsed

Heat the oil in a large skillet over medium-high heat. Add the mushrooms and sear on both sides, then add the shallots and garlic and cook until fragrant, about 30 seconds. Stir in the oregano, basil, wine, lemon juice, parsley, salt, and pepper. Cook for about 2 minutes or until the mushrooms are tender and the liquid is reduced slightly. Add the spinach and continue to cook, stirring to wilt the spinach. Add the beans and cook, stirring occasionally to heat through, about 2 minutes longer. Taste and adjust the seasonings, if needed. Serve hot.

chapter 5

pasta for dinner

When it comes to a quick-fix dinner, the answer, at least in my house, is often pasta. After all, it's easy to cook, economical, nutritious, versatile, and convenient, and it tastes great. Pasta comes in all sizes and shapes, from the tiny *acini di pepe* (peppercorn-shaped pasta) that is used in soups to the conchiglie (large shells) for stuffing. Strand pastas range from the delicate angel hair to the thick perciatelli, along with the ever-popular spaghetti, linguine, and fettuccine. Italian pasta is typically made with semolina flour, but many gluten-free varieties of pasta are also available, and a wide variety of Asian noodles are made with rice.

Adding to the variety inherent in pasta and noodles is the seemingly limitless range of ways to serve them. This chapter features vegan riffs on several classics, including a spaghetti with a hearty Bolognese sauce, linguine with a white clam-ish sauce, and pasta with a creamy avocado Alfredo. Asian noodle recipes include Fire and Ice Sesame Noodles (page 110), Pad Thai Primavera (page 115), and Banh-Mi Noodles (page 111). There are also pasta dishes such as Stroganoff-Inspired Pasta (page 105), Jamaican Rasta Pasta (page 106), and Rotini with Smoky Chickpeas and Cauliflower (page 114) that, while neither Asian nor Italian in origin, are quite simply delicious.

gemelli and rapini with walnut pesto

serves 4

Gemelli is a chewy pasta that pairs well with the bold bite of rapini and the flavorful pesto made with walnuts. The rapini (also known as broccoli rabe) is cooked along with the pasta, and then the pesto is tossed with the pasta and rapini right in the pot, making for easy cleanup.

1 pound gemelli
1 bunch rapini, trimmed and coarsely
    chopped (about 3 cups)
4 cloves garlic, crushed
⅓ cup toasted walnut pieces

½ teaspoon salt
¼ teaspoon red pepper flakes
1 cup fresh basil leaves
3 tablespoons olive oil

Cook the gemelli in a large pot of salted boiling water, stirring occasionally, until it is al dente, about 10 minutes. About halfway through the cooking time, stir in the rapini and continue to cook. Drain well and return the pasta and rapini to the pot.

Meanwhile, combine the garlic, walnuts, and salt in a food processor and process until finely minced. Add the red pepper flakes, basil, and olive oil and process to a paste. Add a little hot pasta water to thin to the desired consistency.

Add the pesto to the pasta and rapini and toss gently to combine. Taste and adjust the seasonings, if needed. Serve hot.

farfalle primavera with fennel sauce

serves 4

With its "butterfly" pasta, colorful fresh vegetables, and creamy fennel sauce, this dish lives up to its "springtime" moniker. Although the ground fennel seed is optional, I highly recommend using it to intensify the flavor of the fresh fennel.

1 pound farfalle
1 tablespoon olive oil or ¼ cup water
1 small yellow onion, chopped
1 large fennel bulb, coarsely chopped
1 teaspoon dried basil
½ teaspoon ground fennel
   seeds (optional)
Salt and freshly ground black pepper

1 red or yellow bell pepper,
   seeded and chopped
1 medium zucchini, chopped
4 ounces white or cremini
   mushrooms, chopped
2 medium fresh tomatoes, chopped
1 cup home-cooked white beans, or
   1 (15.5-ounce) can, drained and rinsed
2 tablespoons chopped fresh basil

Cook the pasta in a large pot of salted boiling water, stirring occasionally, until it is al dente. Drain the pasta and return it to the pot.

Meanwhile, heat the oil in a large skillet over medium heat. Add the onion, chopped fennel, dried basil, ground fennel seed, if using, and salt and pepper to taste. Cover and cook for about 7 minutes to soften. Scoop out the onion and fennel and transfer to a food processor or high-speed blender. Return the skillet to the heat and add the bell pepper, zucchini, mushrooms, and tomatoes. Season with salt and pepper to taste and cook until the vegetables are soft, 8 to 10 minutes.

Add the white beans to the vegetable mixture in the food processor and puree until smooth. Return to the skillet containing the cooked vegetables and keep warm over low heat. Add a little hot pasta water if the sauce becomes too thick.

Add the sauce to the pasta and toss to combine. Sprinkle with the basil and serve hot.

linguine with arugula and cannellini beans

serves 4

Pasta with garlicky greens and beans is a classic for a reason: There aren't many dishes that are easier or more delicious than combining pasta with beans and greens. This version features arugula and cannellini beans with linguine, although you may use another type of pasta instead. Feel free to substitute whatever greens you've got on hand. This is especially nice topped with chopped fresh tomatoes when they're in season or with some toasted pine nuts.

12 ounces linguine
2 tablespoons olive oil or ¼ cup water
4 cloves garlic, minced
½ teaspoon red pepper flakes
½ teaspoon dried basil
½ teaspoon dried oregano
½ teaspoon salt

¼ teaspoon freshly ground black pepper
8 ounces arugula
1½ cups home-cooked cannellini
    beans, or 1 (15.5-ounce) can,
    rinsed and drained
½ cup vegetable broth

Cook the pasta in a large pot of salted boiling water, stirring occasionally, until it is al dente. Drain well and return to the pot.

Meanwhile, heat the oil in a large skillet over medium heat. Add the garlic and cook until fragrant, about 30 seconds. Stir in the red pepper flakes, basil, oregano, salt, and pepper. Add the arugula and cook, stirring to wilt. Stir in the beans and broth and simmer for about 5 minutes to blend the flavors. Keep warm over low heat.

Add the arugula and beans to the cooked pasta and toss gently to combine. Taste and adjust the seasonings, if needed. Serve hot.

Gross

cavatappi and broccoli with creamy artichoke-walnut sauce

serves 4

Cavatappi is a corkscrew-shaped tubular pasta that is also known as celentani; it's available in ridged and smooth versions. It's one of my favorite pasta shapes because of its chewy texture and ability to hold the sauce—in this case, a creamy artichoke-walnut sauce.

8 to 12 ounces cavatappi
4 cups small broccoli florets
1 tablespoon olive oil or ¼ cup water
1 small yellow onion, chopped
3 cloves garlic, chopped
2 tablespoons dry white wine (optional)
1½ cups artichoke hearts (canned
    or thawed cooked), drained
⅓ cup toasted walnut pieces
½ teaspoon salt
Freshly ground black pepper
1 cup hot vegetable broth or
    water, or more if needed
2 tablespoons chopped
    fresh Italian parsley

Cook the cavatappi in a large pot of salted boiling water, stirring occasionally, until it is al dente. About 4 minutes before the pasta is cooked, add the broccoli. Drain the cooked pasta and broccoli well and return to the pot.

Meanwhile, heat the oil in a medium saucepan over medium heat. Add the onion and cook, stirring occasionally, until softened, about 5 minutes. Add the garlic and cook for 1 minute. Stir in the wine, artichoke hearts, walnuts, salt, and pepper to taste and stir to blend the flavors. Transfer the artichoke mixture to a food processor or blender. Add the hot broth and puree until smooth and creamy.

Add the sauce to the pot containing the drained cooked pasta and broccoli and toss gently to combine. Taste and adjust the seasonings, if needed. Serve hot, sprinkled with the parsley.

stroganoff-inspired pasta

serves 4

Serve as is for a creamy mushroom stroganoff, or add seitan for a heartier dish. If you add some cut green beans or broccoli florets when cooking the pasta, you can enjoy this as a one-dish meal.

8 ounces linguine or fettuccine, broken into thirds
1 tablespoon olive oil or ¼ cup water
1 small yellow onion, minced
3 cloves garlic, minced
1 pound mushrooms (any variety), sliced
¼ cup dry white wine
1 teaspoon vegan Worcestershire sauce or tamari soy sauce
1 teaspoon dried thyme
½ teaspoon salt

¼ teaspoon freshly ground black pepper
2 tablespoons nutritional yeast
2 tablespoons cornstarch
1 tablespoon tomato paste
1 teaspoon Dijon mustard
1 cup vegetable broth
2 cups plain unsweetened almond milk or other nondairy milk
½ cup vegan sour cream
3 tablespoons chopped fresh Italian parsley

Cook the pasta in a large pot of boiling salted water until just al dente. Drain and return to the pot.

Meanwhile, heat the oil in a large skillet over medium-high heat. Add the onion and cook until softened, about 5 minutes. Add the garlic and cook for 30 seconds longer. Add the mushrooms and sauté for a few minutes, then stir in the wine, Worcestershire sauce, thyme, salt, and pepper.

In a small saucepan, combine the nutritional yeast, cornstarch, tomato paste, and mustard and mix until blended. Stir in the broth until completely smooth, and heat over medium-high heat. Stir in the almond milk and continue stirring until hot and thickened. Remove from the heat. Stir all but about ½ cup of the sauce into the mushroom mixture. Stir the sour cream into the remaining sauce in the saucepan, then stir it into the sauce in the skillet. Taste and adjust the seasonings, if needed.

Combine the mushroom sauce with the cooked pasta and toss to combine. Serve hot, sprinkled with the parsley.

jamaican rasta pasta

serves 4

Diced butternut squash makes a good addition (you can cook it with the pasta) to this unusual pasta dish that is fragrant with island spices. If you don't want the heat, leave out the hot chile—or add a little more if you like it spicy.

1 tablespoon olive oil or ¼ cup water
3 cloves garlic, minced
1 small fresh hot chile,
   seeded and minced
1 small yellow or red bell pepper,
   seeded and chopped
2 plum tomatoes, chopped
4 scallions, chopped
2 teaspoons grated fresh ginger
1 teaspoon ground coriander
1 teaspoon dried thyme

½ teaspoon ground cumin
½ teaspoon salt
¼ teaspoon freshly ground black pepper
Pinch of allspice
½ cup vegetable broth
¾ cup unsweetened coconut milk
8 to 12 ounces spaghetti
2 to 3 cups small broccoli florets
   or cut green beans
2 tablespoons minced fresh
   Italian parsley or basil

Heat the oil in a saucepan over medium heat. Add the garlic, chile, and bell pepper and cook for 1 minute. Stir in the tomatoes, scallions, ginger, coriander, thyme, cumin, salt, pepper, and allspice. Add the broth and stir in the coconut milk. Simmer for 5 minutes, stirring occasionally, to blend the flavors. Taste and adjust the seasonings, if needed. Keep the sauce warm over low heat.

Cook the spaghetti in a large pot of salted boiling water, stirring occasionally, until it is al dente. About halfway through the cooking process, add the broccoli and cook until tender. Drain well and return to the pot. Add the sauce and toss to combine. Serve hot, sprinkled with the parsley.

linguine with white clam-ish sauce

serves 4

Okay, maybe "clam-ish" isn't actually a word, but it certainly does a good job of describing this sauce inspired by my husband's former personal favorite. Jon used to love white clam sauce so much that for a moment he considered being a "bivalve-mollusk-itarian." Thankfully, I came up with this "clam-ish" sauce so that he could enjoy his favorites and remain a happy vegan.

12 to 16 ounces linguine
2 tablespoons olive oil
5 cloves garlic, minced
2 cups chopped oyster mushrooms
½ teaspoon red pepper flakes
½ teaspoon dried basil
½ teaspoon dried oregano

Salt and freshly ground black pepper
½ cup dry white wine or vegetable broth
⅓ cup chopped fresh parsley
   (either curly or Italian)
¼ cup kalamata olives,
   pitted and chopped
¼ cup toasted pine nuts

Cook the pasta in a pot of boiling salted water until it is just al dente. Drain and return it to the pot.

Meanwhile, heat the oil in a large skillet over medium heat. Add the garlic and cook until fragrant, about 30 seconds. Add the mushrooms and stir in the red pepper flakes, basil, oregano, and salt and pepper to taste. Add the wine and cook, stirring frequently, until the mushrooms are tender, about 5 minutes. Stir in the parsley and olives and keep warm over low heat.

Add the mushroom mixture to the pasta in the pot, and toss to combine. Taste and adjust the seasonings, if needed. Serve hot, sprinkled with the pine nuts.

rotini and asparagus with springtime pesto

serves 4

What says spring better than a "springy" pasta such as rotini? Paired with tender asparagus and a lovely green pesto, it doesn't get springier than this!

8 to 12 ounces rotini
1 pound thin asparagus, trimmed
    and cut into 1-inch pieces
3 tablespoons olive oil
3 cloves garlic, crushed
1 cup fresh Italian parsley
½ cup fresh basil, chervil,
    or tarragon leaves

⅓ cup raw cashews or blanched almonds
⅓ cup fresh or thawed frozen green peas
2 scallions, chopped
¼ cup green olives, pitted
½ teaspoon salt
¼ teaspoon freshly ground black pepper

Cook the pasta in a large pot of salted boiling water, stirring occasionally, until it is al dente. About 4 minutes before the pasta is cooked, add the asparagus and continue cooking.

While the pasta is cooking, heat the oil in a small skillet over medium heat. Add the garlic and cook until softened, about 3 minutes. Transfer the garlic and oil to a high-speed blender. Add the parsley, basil, cashews, peas, scallions, olives, salt, and pepper and process to a paste. Add about ½ cup or more of the hot pasta water to thin and warm the sauce. When the pasta and asparagus are cooked, drain them and return to the pot. Add the pesto and toss gently to combine. Taste and adjust the seasonings, if needed. Serve hot.

creamy sesame soba stir-fry

serves 4

Hearty buckwheat soba noodles stand up nicely to the rich and creamy sesame sauce. Crunchy snow peas and red bell pepper strips add streaks of vibrant color. If you prefer a milder sauce, leave out the chili oil.

8 ounces soba noodles
1 tablespoon neutral vegetable oil
5 scallions, chopped
2 cloves garlic, minced
2 teaspoons grated fresh ginger
1 red bell pepper, seeded and
   cut into thin strips
2 ounces snow peas, trimmed
   and cut into 1-inch pieces

Salt and freshly ground black pepper
3 tablespoons tahini
3 tablespoons tamari soy sauce
2 tablespoons rice vinegar
2 teaspoons natural sugar
1 teaspoon hot chili oil
¼ cup water, or more if needed
1 tablespoon black or toasted
   white sesame seeds

Cook the soba according to the package directions. Drain and set aside.

Heat the oil in a large skillet over medium-high heat. Add the scallions, garlic, and ginger and stir-fry until softened, about 30 seconds. Stir in the bell pepper and snow peas and season with salt and pepper to taste. Stir-fry for 3 minutes, then keep warm over low heat.

In a small bowl, combine the tahini, tamari, vinegar, sugar, chili oil, and water. Mix well to blend. Stir the mixture into the vegetables. Add the cooked soba and stir-fry to coat with the sauce and heat through. Taste and adjust the seasonings, if needed. Serve hot, sprinkled with the sesame seeds.

fire and ice sesame noodles

serves 4

The evocative name refers to the heat from the sriracha and the cold temperature of the dish, since I usually serve it chilled. You can serve it at room temperature, if you prefer, but "fire and room temperature" just doesn't have the same ring to it.

8 to 10 ounces buckwheat soba noodles
1 tablespoon toasted sesame oil
3 scallions, chopped
1 medium carrot, coarsely shredded
½ English cucumber, peeled and chopped
¼ cup tahini
3 tablespoons tamari soy sauce

1 tablespoon white miso paste
1 to 2 teaspoons sriracha sauce
1 teaspoon grated fresh ginger
1 teaspoon natural sugar
1 teaspoon rice vinegar
¼ cup water
2 tablespoons toasted sesame seeds

Cook the soba in a pot of boiling water according to the package directions. Drain well and rinse in cold water, then drain again (extremely well). Return the drained noodles to the pot. Add the sesame oil, scallions, carrot, and cucumber and toss gently to combine. Refrigerate until ready to serve.

In a small bowl, combine the tahini, tamari, miso, sriracha, ginger, sugar, and vinegar. Blend until smooth. Stir in the water and continue stirring until smooth and creamy.

Add the sauce to the noodles and vegetables and toss gently to combine. To serve, transfer the noodles and vegetables to a large serving bowl or individual bowls and top with the sesame seeds.

banh-mi noodles

serves 4

Banh-mi, how do I love thee? Let me count the ways: So far I've made you as the traditional sandwich, a deconstructed salad, and even a pizza. Here, all the flavors of my favorite sandwich are tossed with noodles. Win-win!

8 ounces rice noodles or linguine
2 large carrots, coarsely shredded
1 cucumber, peeled, seeded, and chopped
⅓ cup chopped scallions
2 teaspoons minced fresh ginger
⅓ cup chopped fresh cilantro
2 tablespoons rice vinegar
2 teaspoons toasted sesame oil
2 teaspoons natural sugar

1 tablespoon neutral vegetable oil
8 ounces extra-firm tofu, drained and cut into thin strips
⅓ cup hoisin sauce
3 tablespoons tamari soy sauce
3 tablespoons water
1 to 2 teaspoons sriracha sauce
3 to 4 tablespoons crushed roasted peanuts

Cook the noodles according to the package directions. Drain well and return to the pot. Add the carrots, cucumber, scallions, ginger, cilantro, vinegar, sesame oil, and sugar. Toss to combine and set aside.

Heat the vegetable oil in a large skillet or wok over medium-high heat. Add the tofu and stir-fry quickly to brown it on all sides.

In a small bowl, combine the hoisin, tamari, water, and sriracha, stirring to blend. Pour the sauce mixture onto the tofu and stir-fry for 2 minutes longer. Add the cooked noodle mixture to the tofu mixture and stir-fry until heated through, about 2 minutes longer. Serve hot, sprinkled with the peanuts.

ziti with creamy radicchio sauce

serves 4

"Opulent" is how I would describe this luxurious pasta dish made with radicchio, a member of the chicory family; vegan cream cheese; and smoked paprika. The cream cheese serves to mellow the bitterness inherent in the radicchio as it enriches the sauce.

1 tablespoon olive oil or ¼ cup water
1 small sweet yellow onion, chopped
1 medium head radicchio,
    shredded (about 3 cups)
Salt and freshly ground black pepper
1 teaspoon dried basil
½ teaspoon dried oregano
½ teaspoon smoked paprika
1 cup hot vegetable broth

½ cup vegan cream cheese,
    at room temperature
½ cup plain unsweetened almond
    milk or other nondairy milk
1½ tablespoons freshly
    squeezed lemon juice
1 tablespoon white miso paste
8 ounces ziti
2 tablespoons chopped
    fresh basil (optional)

Heat the oil in a small skillet over medium heat. Add the onion and cook until softened, about 1 minute. Add the radicchio and season with salt and pepper to taste. Cook, stirring to wilt, for about 3 minutes.

Stir in the dried basil, oregano, paprika, and broth. Cover and cook until the radicchio is tender, about 15 minutes. Stir in the cream cheese, almond milk, lemon juice, and miso paste, stirring to blend well. Taste and adjust the seasonings, if needed. For a thinner sauce, add more broth or almond milk. For a thicker sauce, stir in a little extra cream cheese. Keep warm.

While the radicchio is cooking, cook the ziti in a large pot of salted boiling water, stirring occasionally, until it is just al dente. Drain the cooked pasta and return to the pot. Combine the radicchio mixture with the pasta and toss gently to combine. Serve hot, sprinkled with the fresh basil, if using.

fusilli and chickpeas with tomatoes and artichokes

serves 4

This is one of my favorite go-to pasta dishes, and it can be varied according to what you have on hand. I love fusilli for its chewy texture, but any pasta variety can stand in for it. If you don't have mushrooms on hand, leave them out. If you have some zucchini in the house, add it in. If you're not into chickpeas, use cannellini beans. You get the idea.

12 ounces fusilli
1 tablespoon olive oil or ¼ cup water
3 cloves garlic, minced
3 scallions, chopped
4 ounces white or cremini
  mushrooms, thinly sliced
½ teaspoon red pepper flakes
½ teaspoon dried basil
½ teaspoon dried oregano
½ teaspoon salt

¼ teaspoon freshly ground black pepper
2 plum tomatoes, chopped
1 (8-ounce) jar marinated artichoke
  hearts, drained and chopped
1½ cups home-cooked chickpeas, or
  1 (15.5-ounce) can, rinsed and drained
½ cup vegetable broth or dry white wine
2 tablespoons chopped fresh
  Italian parsley or basil

Cook the pasta in a large pot of salted boiling water, stirring occasionally, until it is al dente. Drain well and return to the pot.

Meanwhile, heat the oil in a large skillet over medium heat. Add the garlic and scallions and cook until fragrant, about 30 seconds. Stir in the mushrooms, red pepper flakes, dried basil, oregano, salt, and pepper. Add the tomatoes, artichokes, chickpeas, and broth and cook for 8 to 10 minutes, stirring to break up the tomatoes and blend the flavors.

Combine the chickpea mixture with the cooked pasta and toss gently to combine. Taste and adjust the seasonings, if needed. Serve hot, sprinkled with the parsley.

rotini with smoky chickpeas and cauliflower

serves 4

The smoky chickpeas and cauliflower are so good that you may have a difficult time saving them for this pasta dish. I sometimes make the smoky chickpeas alone and keep them on hand to add to salads or to eat as a snack. They're that good.

2 tablespoons pure maple syrup
2 tablespoons tamari soy sauce
2 tablespoons olive oil
2 teaspoons liquid smoke
2 teaspoons nutritional yeast
1 teaspoon smoked paprika
½ teaspoon salt
¼ teaspoon freshly ground black pepper

1 head cauliflower, chopped
    into small florets
1½ cups home-cooked chickpeas, or
    1 (15.5-ounce) can, rinsed and drained
2 shallots, finely minced
12 ounces rotini
¼ cup minced fresh Italian parsley

Preheat the oven to 425°F. Line two shallow baking dishes with parchment paper or spray them with nonstick cooking spray. In a large bowl, combine the maple syrup, tamari, olive oil, liquid smoke, nutritional yeast, paprika, salt, pepper, cauliflower, chickpeas, and shallots. Toss to combine well.

Transfer the chickpea and cauliflower mixture to the prepared baking dishes and spread in a single layer. Bake for 20 minutes or until the cauliflower is tender, stirring once about halfway through.

While the cauliflower and chickpeas are roasting, cook the rotini in a large pot of salted boiling water until it is al dente. Drain the pasta and return it to the pot. Add a little olive oil and toss to coat. When the cauliflower and chickpeas are done roasting, add them to the pasta, along with the parsley, and toss gently to combine. Serve hot.

pad thai primavera

serves 4

I love the flavor of pad thai, but I always find it to be too long on noodles and too short on vegetables. I remedied that problem with this primavera version of pad thai, loaded with fresh veggies and that same great pad thai flavor. This recipe calls for tamarind sauce, which is much less concentrated than tamarind paste. If you want to use tamarind paste instead, you will only need to use about 1 teaspoon of the paste and dissolve it in hot water before adding it to the dish. If you want to add some heat to this recipe, add a minced hot fresh chile when you add the vegetables, or sprinkle in some red pepper flakes.

8 ounces dried rice noodles
3 tablespoons tamari soy sauce
3 tablespoons water
2 tablespoons tamarind sauce
1 tablespoon rice vinegar
1 tablespoon natural sugar
1 tablespoon neutral vegetable oil
1 small red onion, thinly sliced
3 cloves garlic, minced
2 cups small broccoli florets

1 carrot, thinly sliced
1 red bell pepper, seeded and
  cut into thin strips
4 scallions, chopped
1 cup cherry tomatoes, halved
½ cup fresh bean sprouts
⅓ cup fresh cilantro or Thai basil leaves
¼ cup chopped roasted peanuts
Lime wedges, for serving

Soak the noodles in hot water to soften, 10 to 15 minutes. Drain and set aside.

In a small bowl, combine the tamari, water, tamarind sauce, vinegar, and sugar. Stir to mix well and reserve.

Heat the oil in a large skillet or wok over medium-high heat. Add the onion, garlic, broccoli, carrot, bell pepper, and scallions and stir-fry for 2 minutes to soften the vegetables, adding a tablespoon or so of water so they don't burn. Add the noodles and stir-fry for 1 minute. Add the reserved sauce and stir-fry until the ingredients are hot and coated with the sauce. Serve hot, topped with the tomatoes, sprouts, cilantro, peanuts, and lime wedges.

note: If tamarind is unavailable, add 2 tablespoons of lime juice instead.

lemon-dijon pasta shells with zucchini

serves 4

Creamy and oh-so-yummy, this dish reminds me of a sophisticated cousin of mac and cheese. For a tasty variation, use broccoli instead of zucchini.

8 to 12 ounces medium pasta shells
2 medium zucchini, halved lengthwise
   and cut into ¼-inch slices
1½ cups home-cooked cannellini
   beans, or 1 (15.5-ounce) can,
   drained and rinsed
1 clove garlic, crushed
3 tablespoons nutritional yeast (or
   1 tablespoon white miso paste)

3 tablespoons freshly
   squeezed lemon juice
2 teaspoons Dijon mustard
½ teaspoon salt
¼ teaspoon freshly ground black pepper
¾ cup hot vegetable broth
3 tablespoons chopped fresh
   basil or Italian parsley

Cook the pasta in a large pot of salted boiling water, stirring occasionally, until it is al dente. About 3 minutes before the pasta is done cooking, add the zucchini and continue to cook until done. Drain well and return to the pot.

Meanwhile, combine the cannellini beans, garlic, nutritional yeast, lemon juice, mustard, salt, pepper, and broth in a blender or food processor. Blend until smooth and creamy. Taste and adjust the seasonings, if needed. Add the sauce to the cooked pasta, along with the basil, and toss gently to combine. Serve hot.

pumpkin-sauced penne
with crispy kale

serves 4

Canned solid-pack pumpkin puree is a great ingredient to keep on hand for spontaneous soups, desserts, and pasta sauces like this one. Topped with crispy kale, this dish has "autumn" written all over it. If you want to add more protein to this dish, stir some cooked cannellini beans into the sauce or add some slices of sautéed vegan sausage when ready to serve.

8 ounces kale, stemmed
2 tablespoons olive oil
Salt and freshly ground black pepper
12 ounces penne
2 cloves garlic, minced

2 tablespoons tomato paste
2 teaspoons minced fresh sage
1 teaspoon minced fresh thyme
1 cup canned solid-pack pumpkin
1½ cups vegetable broth

Preheat the oven to 375°F. Tear the kale into bite-size pieces or ¼-inch strips. Toss with 1 tablespoon of the olive oil and arrange on a baking sheet. Season with salt and pepper to taste. Bake until crisp but still tender, about 15 minutes, turning once about halfway through.

While the kale is roasting, cook the pasta in a large pot of salted boiling water, stirring occasionally, until it is al dente. Drain well and return to the pot.

Heat the remaining 1 tablespoon oil in a large skillet over medium heat. Add the garlic and cook until fragrant, about 30 seconds. Stir in the tomato paste, sage, thyme, and pumpkin, then slowly stir in the broth, stirring until well blended. Season with salt and pepper to taste and continue to cook until the sauce is hot and the flavors are blended. Taste and adjust the seasonings, if needed.

Combine the pumpkin mixture with the cooked pasta and toss gently to combine. Serve hot, topped with the crispy kale.

miang kham angel hair and watercress

serves 4

The intense flavors of ginger, coconut, hot chiles, and lime are essential to miang kham, the leaf-wrapped appetizer from Thailand. Those ingredients are transformed into this bold, fresh-tasting main dish made with angel hair pasta and watercress.

¼ cup minced scallions
2 tablespoons finely grated fresh ginger
1 to 2 small fresh Thai chiles,
  cut into very thin rounds
½ cup lightly toasted shredded
  unsweetened coconut
½ cup unsalted roasted peanuts
3 tablespoons tamari soy sauce
2 tablespoons palm sugar or
  other natural sugar

½ cup water
8 ounces angel hair pasta
1 large bunch watercress,
  coarsely chopped
1 carrot, coarsely shredded
2 teaspoons toasted sesame oil
Juice and finely grated zest of 1 lime
⅓ cup chopped fresh cilantro leaves

In a small saucepan, combine the scallions, ginger, chiles, ¼ cup of the coconut, ¼ cup of the peanuts, the tamari, sugar, and water. Bring to a boil, then decrease the heat to low and simmer for 10 minutes to thicken. Remove from the heat and let cool slightly. Transfer to a blender or food processor and blend until smooth.

Cook the pasta in a large pot of salted boiling water until it is al dente. About 2 minutes before the pasta is done cooking, add the watercress and carrot. Drain the pasta and vegetables and return to the pot. Add the sesame oil and lime juice and zest and toss to coat.

Pour the sauce mixture onto the pasta, along with the cilantro and the remaining ¼ cup coconut and ¼ cup peanuts. Toss gently to combine and heat through. Taste and adjust the seasonings, adding additional tamari, if needed. Serve hot.

spaghetti with cremini bolognese sauce

serves 4

Finely chopped cremini mushrooms mimic the texture of ground beef in this flavorful Bolognese sauce that's made rich and creamy with the addition of some vegan cream cheese. This recipe features spaghetti, the traditional pasta paired with Bolognese sauce, but you can substitute any pasta shape you may prefer.

1 tablespoon olive oil
1 medium yellow onion, finely chopped
3 cloves garlic, minced
8 ounces cremini mushrooms,
   finely chopped
3 tablespoons tomato paste
½ teaspoon dried oregano
½ teaspoon dried basil

½ teaspoon red pepper flakes
½ teaspoon natural sugar
1 (28-ounce) can diced tomatoes,
   including juices
Salt and freshly ground black pepper
½ cup vegan cream cheese,
   at room temperature
12 ounces spaghetti

Heat the oil in a large skillet over medium heat. Add the onion and garlic and cook, stirring occasionally, until softened, about 5 minutes. Add the mushrooms and a little water, if needed, so the vegetables do not burn. Cook for 2 minutes longer, then stir in the tomato paste, oregano, basil, red pepper flakes, sugar, tomatoes, and salt and pepper to taste and bring just to a boil. Decrease the heat to low and simmer for 15 minutes or until the sauce has thickened and the flavors have blended. Taste and adjust the seasonings, if needed. Stir in the cream cheese until well blended. Keep warm over low heat.

While the sauce is simmering, cook the spaghetti in a large pot of salted boiling water, stirring occasionally, until it is al dente. To serve, top the pasta with the sauce and serve hot.

rotini with broccoli and creamy sun-dried tomato sauce

serves 4

Sun-dried tomatoes add their unique flavor to this creamy sauce made with white beans and nutritional yeast. Teamed with rotini and broccoli and sprinkled with toasted pine nuts, it makes for an easy and delicious meal.

8 ounces rotini
3 cups small broccoli florets
1 tablespoon olive oil or ¼ cup water
3 cloves garlic, minced
1 cup home-cooked white beans, or
    1 (15.5-ounce) can, drained and rinsed
1 cup vegetable broth
½ cup reconstituted sun-dried
    tomatoes, chopped

2 tablespoons nutritional yeast (or
    1 tablespoon white miso paste)
½ teaspoon dried basil
Salt and freshly ground black pepper
¾ cup plain unsweetened almond
    milk or other nondairy milk
3 tablespoons toasted pine nuts

Cook the rotini in a large pot of salted boiling water, stirring occasionally, until it is just al dente. About halfway through, add the broccoli to the pasta and cook until tender. Drain well and return to the pot.

Meanwhile, heat the oil in a small skillet over medium heat. Add the garlic and cook until fragrant, 30 seconds. Add the beans, broth, tomatoes, nutritional yeast, basil, and salt and pepper to taste and cook for 1 minute longer to blend the flavors. Transfer the mixture to a blender or food processor. Add the almond milk and process until smooth and creamy. Taste and adjust the seasonings, if needed. Add the sauce to the cooked pasta and broccoli and toss to combine. Serve hot, topped with the pine nuts.

farfalle with madeira mushrooms

serves 4

I love the flavor of mushrooms that have been cooked in Madeira, a fortified wine with a distinctive sweet flavor. If unavailable, you can substitute dry sherry, white wine, or vegetable broth—the flavor will be different, but it will still be delicious. I highly recommend adding the optional sour cream at the end to enrich the sauce.

12 ounces farfalle
1 tablespoon olive oil
2 shallots, minced
3 cloves garlic, minced
8 ounces cremini mushrooms, chopped
8 ounces white mushrooms, sliced
½ cup Madeira (see headnote)
1 (14.5-ounce) can diced tomatoes, drained (or 2 medium fresh tomatoes, chopped)

1 tablespoon tamari soy sauce
½ teaspoon dried thyme
½ teaspoon dried dill weed
Salt and freshly ground black pepper
1 teaspoon cornstarch dissolved in 1 tablespoon water
½ cup vegan sour cream (optional)
2 tablespoons chopped fresh Italian parsley

Cook the farfalle in a pot of boiling salted water until just al dente. Drain and return to the pot.

Meanwhile, heat the oil in a large skillet or saucepan over medium heat. Add the shallots and garlic and cook until softened, about 1 minute. Stir in both kinds of mushrooms, then add the Madeira and cook, stirring, for 2 minutes. Stir in the tomatoes, tamari, thyme, dill, and salt and pepper to taste. Cook, stirring occasionally, until the mushrooms are tender, about 5 minutes. Pour in the cornstarch mixture and stir to thicken slightly. Just before serving, stir in the sour cream, if using, and parsley.

To serve, either combine the mushroom mixture with the farfalle and toss to mix well or divide the pasta among serving plates or shallow bowls and top each with a portion of the mushrooms. Serve hot.

penne and cannellini beans with fennel and olives

serves 4

If you haven't used fennel in your cooking, this is a good place to start. Its mild flavor is complemented here by the creamy white beans and bold kalamata olives. If fresh fennel is unavailable, zucchini is also great in this recipe.

8 ounces penne
1 tablespoon olive oil
1 small red onion, finely chopped
1 large or 2 small fennel bulbs, trimmed and thinly sliced (about 3 cups)
1 large fresh tomato, chopped
1½ cups home-cooked cannellini beans, or 1 (15.5-ounce) can, drained and rinsed

⅓ cup kalamata olives, pitted and chopped
2 tablespoons freshly squeezed lemon juice
Salt and freshly ground black pepper
1 tablespoon minced fresh tarragon or basil

Cook the pasta in a large pot of boiling salted water until it is al dente. Drain well and return to the pot.

Meanwhile, heat the oil in a large skillet over medium heat. Add the onion and fennel and sauté for about 5 minutes to soften. Stir in the tomato, beans, olives, lemon juice, and salt and pepper to taste. Mix well and cook for a few minutes longer to heat through. Stir in the tarragon, then taste and adjust the seasonings, if needed.

To serve, either add the fennel mixture to the pasta and toss to combine or divide the pasta among serving plates or shallow bowls and top each with a portion of the fennel mixture.

pumpkin mac uncheese

serves 4

Super-speedy and nutritious, this tasty interpretation of stovetop mac and cheese is destined to become a family favorite. Add some thawed frozen peas or cooked small broccoli florets if you have some on hand.

8 to 12 ounces rotini
1 cup canned solid-pack pumpkin
¼ cup nutritional yeast
1 tablespoon cornstarch or
   arrowroot powder

2 teaspoons Dijon mustard
1 cup plain unsweetened almond
   milk or other nondairy milk
Salt and freshly ground black pepper
⅓ cup ground toasted walnuts

Cook the rotini in a pot of boiling salted water until it is al dente. Drain and return to the pot.

In a saucepan, combine the pumpkin, nutritional yeast, cornstarch, mustard, almond milk, and salt and pepper to taste. Stir constantly over medium heat until the sauce is well blended and begins to thicken, about 5 minutes.

Combine the cooked pasta with the sauce, and stir gently to mix thoroughly. Serve topped with the ground walnuts.

meal-worthy sandwiches

Sandwiches are the quintessential fast food, making them an ideal candidate for a quick-fix meal. Still, there are some who might question the need for a chapter devoted to sandwiches. After all, anybody can slap something between two slices of bread, right? Well, the recipes in this chapter are above and beyond your average lunch box special. I call them "meal-worthy" sandwiches because they are just that—hearty, flavorful, and special enough to enjoy not just for lunch, but for dinner as well.

Here you will find new spins on old favorites, such as Sloppy Jacks (page 127), sloppy Joes made with canned jackfruit; Taste of the Chickpea Sandwiches (page 134), a vegan tuna sandwich; and Seitan Shawarmas (page 128), that luscious pita-wrapped sandwich made vegan with seitan.

There are also unique combinations such as Tonkatsu Tacos (page 137), Smoky Tofu Caesar Wraps (page 139), Sriracha Eggless Salad Sandwiches with Avocado (page 129), and many more. So get out the napkins and grab a bag of chips, because there's a whole lot of sandwiches going on.

sloppy jacks

serves 4

This latest incarnation of the popular sloppy Joe features jackfruit, hence the name Sloppy Jacks! Look for canned water-packed jackfruit in Asian markets or well-stocked supermarkets (be sure not to get the kind packed in syrup). If jackfruit is unavailable, substitute your choice of chopped seitan, steamed crumbled tempeh, chopped mushrooms, or reconstituted TVP.

1 tablespoon olive oil

1 medium yellow onion, minced

3 cloves garlic, minced

1 small red bell pepper,
   seeded and chopped

1 (16-ounce) can water-packed jackfruit,
   drained and shredded or thinly sliced

1 cup tomato sauce

⅓ cup barbecue sauce

2 tablespoons pure maple syrup

1 tablespoon tamari soy sauce

2 teaspoons yellow mustard

1 teaspoon chili powder

½ teaspoon smoked paprika

½ teaspoon liquid smoke

½ teaspoon salt

¼ teaspoon freshly ground black pepper

4 sandwich rolls, split and toasted

Heat the oil in a saucepan over medium heat. Add the onion, garlic, and bell pepper and cook until softened, 5 minutes. Stir in the jackfruit and cook for 2 minutes longer. Stir in the tomato sauce, barbecue sauce, maple syrup, tamari, mustard, chili powder, paprika, liquid smoke, salt, and pepper. Cook, stirring occasionally to heat through and blend the flavors, for about 7 minutes.

Mix well, adding a little water if the mixture is too dry. Simmer for 5 minutes longer to blend flavors. When ready to serve, spoon the mixture onto the rolls and serve hot.

Pretty good

seitan shawarmas

serves 4

Similar to the Greek gyro sandwich, a shawarma is a hearty sandwich found throughout the Middle East. This vegan version features thinly sliced seitan that gets wrapped in pita bread with a garlicky mayo and sliced tomatoes, onions, and cucumbers. Sliced avocado makes quite a nice addition as well.

2 cloves garlic, chopped
½ cup vegan mayonnaise
3 tablespoons freshly
   squeezed lemon juice
Salt and freshly ground black pepper
1 tablespoon olive oil
8 ounces seitan, very thinly sliced

1 teaspoon dried oregano
4 warm pitas or other flatbreads, warmed
1 cup shredded lettuce
1 large fresh tomato, halved
   and thinly sliced
½ red onion, thinly sliced
½ English cucumber, peeled and chopped

In a food processor or blender, combine the garlic, mayonnaise, 2 tablespoons of the lemon juice, and salt and pepper to taste. Process until well blended and then transfer to a bowl. Taste and adjust the seasonings, if needed, and set aside.

Heat the oil in a skillet over medium heat. Add the seitan and cook until browned, about 5 minutes. Add the oregano and the remaining 1 tablespoon lemon juice and season with salt and pepper to taste, tossing to coat.

To assemble, spread the reserved mayonnaise onto the pita loaves, divide the seitan mixture among them, and top with the lettuce, tomato, onion, and cucumber. Serve immediately.

sriracha eggless salad sandwiches with avocado

serves 4

Chickpeas and tofu team up to make a fabulous vegan "egg" salad. Celery, carrot, and scallions add a refreshing crunch, while creamy avocado and spicy sriracha provide a flavor profile that is off-the-charts delicious.

1 cup home-cooked chickpeas, or
   1 (15.5-ounce) can, drained and rinsed
8 ounces extra-firm tofu,
   drained and crumbled
½ cup minced celery
⅓ cup finely shredded carrot
2 scallions, finely minced
1 Hass avocado, pitted,
   peeled, and chopped

½ cup vegan mayonnaise
1½ teaspoons sriracha sauce
1 tablespoon freshly squeezed
   lemon or lime juice
Salt and freshly ground black pepper
8 slices bread or 4 pita loaves
   or other flatbread
4 lettuce leaves

Place the chickpeas in a large bowl and mash well. Add the tofu, celery, carrot, scallions, and avocado and mash to combine. Add the mayonnaise, sriracha, lemon juice, and salt and pepper to taste. Mix well to combine thoroughly. Taste and adjust the seasonings, if needed.

To assemble, spoon the mixture onto 4 slices of the bread. Top with the lettuce and the remaining bread slices. (Roll up the sandwiches if using flatbread.) Serve immediately.

curried chickpea pitas

serves 4

Sweet bits of apple and cranberry mingle with crunchy nuts and celery, creamy chickpeas, and a luscious curry dressing for textures and flavors that really pop. I especially like using coconut vegan yogurt for the dressing, but if you don't have any you can use vegan mayo instead. I like a soft leaf lettuce in these sandwiches, but crunchy romaine or even iceberg works well too.

½ cup coconut vegan yogurt,
    or more if needed
1½ teaspoons curry powder
1 tablespoon agave nectar
1 teaspoon freshly squeezed lemon juice
¼ teaspoon salt
3 cups home-cooked chickpeas, or
    2 (15.5-ounce) cans, drained and rinsed

½ cup chopped celery
⅓ cup chopped cashews,
    almonds, or peanuts
⅓ cup dried sweetened cranberries
    or golden raisins
1 Fuji or Gala apple, cored and chopped
Lettuce leaves (any type)
4 pita loaves, halved

In a large bowl, combine the yogurt, curry powder, agave, lemon juice, and salt, stirring to blend well. Add the chickpeas, celery, cashews, cranberries, and apple and stir to combine well and coat the ingredients with the yogurt dressing. If the mixture is too dry, stir in a little more yogurt. Taste and adjust the seasonings, if needed.

To assemble, stuff a lettuce leaf or two into each pita half and spoon some of the chickpea mixture inside. Serve immediately.

pan-seared portobellos on toast

serves 4

This sandwich was vaguely inspired by the open-face creamed chipped beef on toast of the early twentieth century that was infamously known by its military slang name of "SOS," aka "s**t on a shingle." This updated (and much more appetizing) version is made with thinly sliced portobello mushrooms and a flavorful sauce spiked with smoked paprika and Dijon mustard. For a nice flavor variation, use some fresh shiitakes or other type of mushrooms for a portion of the portobellos.

1 tablespoon olive oil
4 to 5 large portobello mushroom
  caps, gills scraped out,
  halved, then thinly sliced
3 scallions, minced
1 teaspoon dried thyme
½ teaspoon smoked paprika
¼ teaspoon freshly ground black pepper
2 tablespoons tamari soy sauce

½ teaspoon Dijon mustard
½ cup plain unsweetened almond
  milk or other nondairy milk
1 teaspoon cornstarch dissolved
  in 2 tablespoons water
4 slices bread (any kind)
2 tablespoons chopped
  fresh Italian parsley

Heat the oil in a large skillet over medium-high heat. Add the portobellos and stir-fry until nicely seared all over. Add the scallions and cook for 1 minute, then sprinkle the mushrooms with the thyme, paprika, black pepper, and tamari. Stir in the mustard and almond milk, then stir in the cornstarch mixture, stirring until the sauce is thickened. Keep warm while you toast the bread.

Once the bread is toasted, cut the slices in half and arrange them on plates. Top with the mushroom mixture and sprinkle with the parsley. Serve hot.

philly uncheesesteaks

serves 4

What's better than a Philly cheesesteak? Why, a Philly UnCheesesteak, of course. Made with thinly sliced seitan, mushrooms, onions, and bell peppers, and topped with vegan cheddar and enveloped in a crusty baguette, this is one hearty sandwich. If you prefer not to use store-bought vegan cheddar, you can instead drizzle on some homemade Cheesy Sauce.

1 tablespoon olive oil
1 medium yellow onion, thinly sliced
4 ounces seitan, thinly sliced
4 portobello mushroom
   caps, thinly sliced
1 red bell pepper, seeded
   and thinly sliced
2 tablespoons ketchup

1 tablespoon vegan Worcestershire sauce
Salt and freshly ground black pepper
6 slices vegan cheddar or ¾ cup
   shredded vegan cheddar cheese
   or Cheesy Sauce (recipe follows)
1 French baguette, cut into quarters,
   each quarter sliced lengthwise

Heat the oil in a large skillet over medium-high heat. Add the onion, seitan, mushrooms, and bell pepper and stir-fry to soften, about 5 minutes. Stir in the ketchup and Worcestershire sauce and season with salt and pepper to taste. Continue to cook for 5 to 7 minutes longer, until the vegetables are very soft. Spread the cheese on top to allow it to melt into the vegetable and seitan mixture.

Lightly toast the baguette pieces, if desired. Divide the vegetable and seitan mixture among the baguette sections and serve.

cheesy sauce
makes about 4 cups

1 russet potato, peeled and
  cut into 1-inch dice
1 cup vegetable broth
½ roasted red bell pepper
½ cup nutritional yeast
2 tablespoons tahini
1 teaspoon white miso paste
½ teaspoon Dijon mustard
½ teaspoon ground turmeric
½ teaspoon onion powder
1 cup unsweetened almond milk
  or other nondairy milk
1 tablespoon rice vinegar
Salt
1 tablespoon cornstarch dissolved in
  2 tablespoons water (optional)

Combine the potato and broth in a small saucepan. Cover and cook until the potato is tender, 10 to 12 minutes. Transfer the mixture to a high-speed blender or food processor. Add the roasted bell pepper, nutritional yeast, tahini, miso, mustard, turmeric, onion powder, almond milk, vinegar, and salt to taste. Process until well blended. For a thinner sauce, add more liquid and adjust the seasonings as desired. For a thicker sauce, transfer to a saucepan and bring just to a boil, stir in 1 tablespoon cornstarch blended into 2 tablespoons of water, and stir until thickened. Store leftovers in the refrigerator in a tightly sealed container for up to 5 days.

taste of the chickpea sandwiches

serves 4

A few shakes of Old Bay Seasoning and nori flakes add the taste of the sea to these chickpea sandwiches that are a tasty alternative to tuna salad sandwiches. Small shakers of nutrient-rich nori, dulse, and other dried sea vegetables can be found in natural food stores, or look for vegan furikake (made without bonito) in Asian markets. Another alternative is to use scissors to snip tiny pieces from a sheet of nori.

3 cups home-cooked chickpeas, or
   2 (15.5-ounce) cans, drained and rinsed
2 celery ribs, cut into 2-inch pieces
3 scallions, chopped
½ cup vegan mayonnaise
1½ to 2 tablespoons freshly
   squeezed lemon juice
1 teaspoon spicy brown mustard
1 teaspoon nori, dulse, or other sea
   vegetable flakes (see headnote)

½ teaspoon vegan Worcestershire sauce
2 tablespoons minced fresh
   Italian parsley
½ teaspoon Old Bay Seasoning
½ teaspoon salt
¼ teaspoon freshly ground black pepper
8 slices bread (any type)
4 lettuce leaves (any variety)
4 slices fresh tomato
Hot sauce, for serving (optional)

In a food processor, combine the chickpeas, celery, and scallions and pulse until coarsely broken up. Set aside.

In a bowl, combine the mayonnaise, lemon juice, mustard, nori flakes, Worcestershire sauce, parsley, Old Bay, salt, and pepper and stir until well blended. Add the chickpea mixture and mix to combine. Taste and adjust the seasonings, if needed. Scoop out the mixture and divide into 4 equal portions.

To assemble, toast the bread, if desired, then divide the chickpea mixture among 4 slices of the bread. Top each with lettuce, tomato, and another slice of bread. Cut the sandwiches diagonally and serve immediately, with hot sauce, if using, on the side.

hoppin' john po'boys

serves 4

This recipe combines two Southern classics: the famed combo of rice and black-eyed peas made into tasty little patties to stuff into a New Orleans po'boy sandwich. If Creole mustard is unavailable, substitute a spicy brown mustard.

1 clove garlic, crushed

3 scallions, chopped

1½ cups home-cooked black-eyed peas, or 1 (15.5-ounce) can, well drained and blotted dry

1 cup cooked brown rice

⅓ cup old-fashioned rolled oats

1 teaspoon Cajun spice blend

3 tablespoons Creole mustard

Salt and freshly ground black pepper

2 tablespoons olive oil

2 tablespoons vegan mayonnaise

1 French baguette, cut into quarters, or 4 small sub rolls

2 cups shredded lettuce

1 large fresh tomato, thinly sliced

Pickled sliced jalapeños, for serving (optional)

Tabasco or other hot sauce, for serving

In a food processor, combine the garlic and scallions and process until finely minced. Add the black-eyed peas, rice, oats, spice blend, 1 tablespoon of the mustard, and salt and pepper to taste and process until well mixed. Pinch the mixture to be sure it holds together. If it is too moist, add additional oats and process until the mixture holds together well. Shape the mixture into twelve 1½-inch balls and press them down with the palm of your hand to make small patties.

Heat the oil in a large skillet over medium heat. Add the patties and cook until nicely browned, then flip over and cook the other side until browned, about 4 minutes per side.

To assemble the sandwiches, spread the mayonnaise and the remaining 2 tablespoons mustard on the inside top and bottom of the bread. Spread some lettuce onto the bottom of each sandwich, followed by tomato slices. Top with the hoppin' John patties (3 per sandwich) and a few slices of jalapeños, if using. Serve immediately, with Tabasco on the side.

beans and greens burritos

serves 4

The quintessential combo of beans and greens makes a yummy and nutritious burrito filling. Instead of (or in addition to) the vegan cheese (or Cheesy Sauce), you could add your favorite burrito toppings, such as avocado, sour cream, or chopped scallions.

1 tablespoon olive oil
1 small yellow onion, minced
2 cloves garlic, minced
8 ounces coarsely chopped
   spinach, chard, or kale
2 cups home-cooked pinto beans, or
   1 (15.5-ounce) can, drained and rinsed

½ cup tomato salsa
1 teaspoon chili powder
½ teaspoon salt
¼ teaspoon freshly ground black pepper
4 (10-inch) flour tortillas, warmed
½ to 1 cup shredded vegan cheese
   or Cheesy Sauce (page 133)

Heat the oil in a large saucepan over medium heat. Add the onion and garlic and cook until softened, 5 minutes. Add the spinach and stir until wilted, then stir in the beans, salsa, and chili powder, stirring to combine and heat through. Use the back of a fork to mash some of the beans as they cook. Season with the salt and pepper.

To serve, spoon one-quarter of the mixture down the center of one of the tortillas. Top the mixture with one-quarter of the cheese. Roll up into a burrito, tucking in the sides as you roll. Repeat with the remaining ingredients. Serve immediately or place the filled burritos (one at a time) in a hot nonstick skillet for a minute or two—just long enough to lightly brown the outside of the tortillas.

tonkatsu tacos

serves 4

East meets West in these flavor-packed tacos made with a tangy and crisp Asian slaw and Japanese tonkatsu-style sauce made with ginger, soy sauce, chili sauce, and apple juice. Stir-fried seitan makes a healthy and delicious alternative to the breaded pork cutlets used to make traditional tonkatsu.

4 cups finely shredded cabbage
1 carrot, finely shredded
2 tablespoons rice vinegar
1½ teaspoons natural sugar
½ teaspoon toasted sesame oil
Salt and freshly ground black pepper
2 tablespoons olive oil
½ cup chopped red onion
12 ounces seitan or extra-firm
   tofu (pressed if using tofu),
   cut into ¼-inch strips

2 cloves garlic, minced
1 teaspoon grated fresh ginger
¼ cup tamari soy sauce
1 tablespoon agave nectar
1 tablespoon sweet Thai chili sauce
1 teaspoon spicy brown mustard
¼ cup apple juice
8 small flour tortillas or taco shells

In a large bowl, combine the cabbage, carrot, rice vinegar, sugar, and sesame oil. Season with salt and pepper to taste and toss to mix well. Set aside.

Heat 1 tablespoon of the olive oil in a skillet over medium heat. Add the onion and cook until softened, 4 minutes. Add the seitan, garlic, and ginger and stir-fry for 2 minutes. Stir in the tamari, agave, chili sauce, mustard, and apple juice. Cook, stirring, to coat and blend the flavors and reduce the sauce by about one-third. Taste and adjust the seasonings, if needed.

To serve, spread one-eighth of the seitan mixture down the center of a tortilla. Top with a portion of the slaw, then roll up. Repeat with the remaining ingredients.

burgers with the works

serves 4 to 6

Made with walnuts, oats, and cooked lentils, these are the burgers to make when you want a tasty, hearty veggie burger that will stand up to "the works." Serve with a side of slaw, potato chips, or fries.

½ cup walnut pieces
½ cup old-fashioned rolled oats
¼ cup chopped yellow onion
1½ cups home-cooked lentils or
    black beans, or 1 (15.5-ounce)
    can, drained and rinsed
¼ cup vital wheat gluten flour
2 tablespoons tamari soy sauce
½ teaspoon smoked paprika

½ teaspoon salt
¼ teaspoon freshly ground black pepper
Olive oil, for frying
4 to 6 lettuce leaves (any kind)
4 to 6 slices fresh tomato
4 to 6 burger rolls, split and toasted
8 to 12 slices pickle chips
Ketchup, mustard, and/or
    relish, for serving

In a food processor, combine the walnuts, oats, and onion and pulse until coarsely ground. Add the lentils, vital wheat gluten flour, tamari, paprika, salt, and pepper. Process until well combined but with some texture remaining.

Shape the mixture into 4 to 6 patties, about 4 inches in diameter, adding a little more vital wheat gluten flour if the mixture is too wet.

Heat a thin layer of oil in a large skillet over medium heat. Add the burgers and cook until browned on both sides, turning once, about 4 minutes per side. To serve, arrange a lettuce leaf and tomato slice on the bottom half of each roll. Top each with a burger and 2 or 3 pickle chips. Serve immediately with ketchup, mustard, and/or relish.

smoky tofu caesar wraps

We'd eat it again!

serves 4 to 6

If you enjoy a good vegan Caesar salad, then you'll love this "salad wrap" with smoky tofu, crisp lettuce, and a creamy, garlicky Caesar dressing made with cashews. For an even quicker version, use a package of ready-made baked marinated tofu.

3 tablespoons neutral vegetable oil
12 to 16 ounces extra-firm tofu, drained and cut into ¼-inch strips
2 tablespoons tamari soy sauce
1 tablespoon rice vinegar
1 tablespoon agave nectar
1 teaspoon liquid smoke
½ cup raw cashews, soaked in water for 3 hours or overnight
2 cloves garlic, crushed
¼ cup nutritional yeast

3 tablespoons freshly squeezed lemon juice
1 teaspoon yellow mustard
½ teaspoon salt
1 Hass avocado
4 to 6 (10-inch) flour tortillas or other flatbread
1 carrot, finely shredded
1 cup finely shredded lettuce
1 fresh tomato, thinly sliced

Heat 1 tablespoon of the oil in a large skillet over medium heat. Add the tofu and cook until golden brown, turning frequently, about 10 minutes. Add the tamari, vinegar, agave, and liquid smoke, stirring gently to coat the tofu. Remove from the heat and set aside to cool.

Drain the cashews. In a high-speed blender or food processor, combine the garlic, cashews, and nutritional yeast and grind to a paste. Add the lemon juice, mustard, salt, and the remaining 2 tablespoons oil and process until smooth.

To assemble the wraps, halve and pit the avocado. Scoop out the flesh with a spoon and chop. Arrange one-quarter of the tofu strips down the center of each tortilla. Top with the carrot, lettuce, tomato, and avocado, then spoon on as much of the dressing as desired. Roll up each wrap tightly and serve at once.

artichoke, white bean, and green olive quesadillas

serves 4

This Italian take on quesadillas combines cannellini beans, olives, and artichoke hearts. Enjoy as is or serve with a small bowl of warm marinara sauce for dipping.

1 (8-ounce) jar marinated
    artichoke hearts, drained
1½ cups home-cooked cannellini
    beans, or 1 (15.5-ounce) can,
    drained and rinsed
½ cup green olives, pitted
2 scallions, chopped

2 tablespoons chopped fresh
    basil or Italian parsley
Salt and freshly ground black pepper
4 (10-inch) flour tortillas
    or other flatbread
1 cup warm marinara sauce (optional)

In a food processor, combine the artichoke hearts, beans, olives, scallions, basil, and salt and pepper to taste. Process to finely chop and mix well.

Arrange the tortillas on a flat work surface. Divide the mixture among the tortillas and spread evenly. Fold the tortillas over, pressing down to hold them together.

Heat a large nonstick skillet over medium heat. Add one or two of the quesadillas (depending on the size of your pan) and cook until golden brown on one side, about 2 minutes. Carefully flip over and brown the other side, about 1 minute longer. Keep the quesadillas warm while you cook the rest. Serve hot, with a bowl of warm marinara sauce, if using, on the side.

super salad wraps with red pepper–white bean spread

serves 4

This simple but satisfying lunch combines a zesty red pepper and white bean spread with an assortment of fresh vegetables, creamy avocado, and piquant artichoke hearts and green olives.

1 large roasted red bell pepper
　(page 20), or 1 (6-ounce) jar,
　well drained and blotted dry
1½ cups home-cooked cannellini
　beans, or 1 (15.5-ounce) can,
　drained and rinsed
Salt and freshly ground black pepper
2 cups shredded romaine lettuce
2 medium fresh tomatoes, chopped
1 carrot, finely shredded

1 English cucumber, peeled and chopped
2 scallions, minced
1 Hass avocado, pitted,
　peeled, and chopped
1 (8-ounce) jar marinated artichoke
　hearts, drained and chopped
⅓ cup green olives, pitted and chopped
4 (10-inch) flour tortillas
　or other flatbread

In a food processor, combine the bell pepper, white beans, and salt and pepper to taste. Process until smooth. Set aside.

In a bowl, combine the lettuce, tomatoes, carrot, cucumber, scallions, avocado, artichoke hearts, and olives. Season with salt and pepper to taste and toss to combine well.

To assemble, spread the reserved red pepper–white bean spread on the surface of each tortilla. Top each with the salad mixture. Roll up each wrap tightly, cut in half, and serve immediately.

veracruz tacos

serves 4

Reminiscent of Baja-style tacos, but without the fish, these tacos combine crunchy cabbage slaw and creamy avocado with strips of sautéed tofu seasoned with nori flakes, chili powder, and nutritional yeast. Be sure to warm the taco shells before serving to get the most flavor from them.

½ cup vegan sour cream
⅓ cup chopped fresh cilantro leaves
2 tablespoons freshly squeezed lime juice
1 teaspoon hot sauce, plus
   more for serving
½ teaspoon yellow mustard
½ teaspoon ground cumin
2 cups finely shredded cabbage
Salt and freshly ground black pepper
2 tablespoons nutritional yeast

2 tablespoons cornstarch
1 teaspoon nori flakes or kelp granules
½ teaspoon chili powder
1 tablespoon olive oil
1 pound extra-firm tofu, drained
   and cut into strips
1 Hass avocado
8 taco shells, warmed
1 lime, cut into wedges

In a large bowl, combine the sour cream, cilantro, lime juice, hot sauce, mustard, and cumin and mix well. Add the cabbage and salt and pepper to taste. Mix well and set aside.

In a shallow bowl, combine the nutritional yeast, cornstarch, nori flakes, chili powder, ½ teaspoon salt, and ¼ teaspoon pepper. Stir to mix.

Heat the oil in a large nonstick skillet over medium-high heat. Dredge the tofu in the spice mixture and add to the hot skillet. Cook the tofu until nicely browned all over, turning as needed, 8 to 10 minutes total.

To assemble, halve and pit the avocado. Scoop out the flesh with a spoon and chop. Spoon some of the slaw into the warmed taco shells and top with several strips of the tofu and a couple of strips of avocado. Serve immediately, with the lime wedges and extra hot sauce.

mediterranean portobello wraps with peperoncini spread

serves 4

The flavorful spread in these wraps features the popular Italian or Greek pickled peperoncini peppers, widely available on supermarket shelves. Consider adding strips of zucchini or yellow summer squash when you sauté the mushrooms.

1 tablespoon olive oil
1 large red onion, thinly sliced
4 large portobello mushroom
   caps, cut into thin strips
3 cloves garlic, minced
1 roasted red bell pepper, cut into strips
½ teaspoon dried basil
½ teaspoon dried oregano
Salt and freshly ground black pepper

1½ cups home-cooked white beans, or
   1 (15.5-ounce) can, drained and rinsed
⅓ cup jarred peperoncini
   peppers, stemmed
2 tablespoons reconstituted or oil-
   packed sun-dried tomatoes, chopped
4 (10-inch) flour tortillas
   or other flatbread
2 cups thinly sliced romaine lettuce
2 plum tomatoes, thinly sliced

Heat the oil in a large skillet over medium heat. Add the onion and cook until softened, 5 minutes. Add the mushrooms and garlic and continue to cook until the mushrooms are soft, 5 minutes longer. Stir in the bell pepper, basil, oregano, and salt and pepper to taste. Remove from the heat and set aside.

In a food processor, combine the beans, peperoncini, and sun-dried tomatoes. Process until smooth.

To assemble, spread the peperoncini mixture on the surface of each tortilla. Top each with one-quarter of the portobello mixture. Top with some lettuce and tomatoes. Roll up each wrap tightly, cut in half, and serve immediately.

"pantry makes perfect" recipes

Sometimes our schedules can be so hectic that we don't even have time to go to the store for fresh produce or other ingredients to make dinner. It's nights like that when we might be tempted to order takeout or maybe just have a bowl of cereal for dinner. What if there were other solutions? Because, there are—and they are as close as your own pantry.

The recipes in this chapter use only pantry ingredients, so if you keep these ingredients on hand, there can always something cooking for dinner, even when there's nothing in the fridge or freezer.

These pantry recipes include a delectable Curried Red Bean and Pumpkin Soup (page 154), Pantry Burgers (page 153), and hearty main dishes such as Pantry Paella (page 148) and Three-Bean Pantry Chili (page 147). And for those times when you want something sweet but don't have the time for from-scratch baking, there are even a few "pantry-perfect" dessert recipes.

three-bean pantry chili

serves 4

A selection of canned beans combined with a jar of salsa and some chili powder are combined here for an almost effortless pot of chili. Vary the beans according to what's on hand (lentils are great in this!), and add some TVP if you like. The optional corn kernels make a tasty addition. Naturally, if you have any chili toppings, such as avocado, scallions, or vegan sour cream, feel free to use them at will.

1 (15.5-ounce) can black beans, drained and rinsed

1 (15.5-ounce) can dark red kidney beans, drained and rinsed

1 (15.5-ounce) can pinto beans, drained and rinsed

1 (24-ounce) jar salsa (hot or mild)

2 to 3 tablespoons chili powder

1 (8-ounce) can corn kernels, drained (optional)

Combine all of the ingredients in a saucepan, reserving half the corn. Cook over medium heat, stirring occasionally, for 15 to 20 minutes, until heated through and any raw taste from the chili powder is cooked away. Add up to 1 cup of water if the chili is too thick. Serve hot, garnished with the remaining corn kernels.

pantry paella

serves 4

Quinoa or quick-cooking rice keeps the cooking time to a minimum in this speedy version of paella. For an even quicker fix, substitute cooked rice or quinoa if you have it on hand (and leave out the water). If you have seitan or soy curls, they'd make a good addition, as would vegan sausage or tempeh.

2 tablespoons olive oil
2 cloves garlic, minced
¾ cup quinoa, well rinsed and drained, or quick-cooking brown rice
1 to 1½ cups water or vegetable broth
1 (28-ounce) can diced tomatoes, including juices
1 (15.5-ounce) can chickpeas, drained and rinsed
1 (8-ounce) jar marinated artichoke hearts, drained and chopped

½ cup sliced pimiento-stuffed green olives
¼ cup reconstituted or oil-packed sun-dried tomatoes
2 teaspoons capers, drained
1 teaspoon dried basil
½ teaspoon dried thyme
Salt and freshly ground black pepper
1 cup frozen green peas

Heat the oil in a large saucepan over medium heat. Add the garlic and cook until fragrant, 30 seconds. Stir in the quinoa, 1 cup of the water, and the diced tomatoes and bring to a boil. Lower the heat to medium, cover, and simmer for 15 minutes.

Stir in the chickpeas, artichoke hearts, olives, sun-dried tomatoes, capers, basil, thyme, and salt and pepper to taste. If the mixture seems dry, add the remaining ½ cup water. Stir in the peas and cook until hot, about 5 minutes.

perfect pantry pasta

serves 4

Sure, a jarred pasta sauce is easier, but if you feel like improvising your own from-scratch tomato sauce, it's easy to do with just a few pantry ingredients. When you combine canned crushed tomatoes with sautéed garlic, some red wine, and herbs, you'll have a "homemade" sauce in minutes. I like to add kalamata olives for extra flavor and texture, but if you're not a fan, consider adding some sliced mushrooms when you sauté the garlic.

1 tablespoon olive oil
3 cloves garlic, chopped
¼ to ½ teaspoon red pepper flakes
2 teaspoons dried basil
1 teaspoon dried oregano
⅓ cup dry red wine

1 (28-ounce) can crushed tomatoes
Salt and freshly ground black pepper
½ cup kalamata olives, pitted
    and chopped (optional)
8 to 12 ounces pasta of choice

Heat the oil in a large saucepan over medium heat. Add the garlic and cook until fragrant, 30 seconds. Stir in the red pepper flakes, basil, and oregano. Stir in the wine and tomatoes and season to taste with salt and pepper. Simmer for 15 minutes, stirring occasionally. Stir in the olives, if using.

Cook the pasta in a pot of boiling salted water until just al dente. Drain well. Serve the hot pasta topped with the sauce.

artichoke-walnut couscous "quiche"

serves 4

This easy recipe isn't a quiche in the traditional sense, but it gets baked in a quiche pan, pie plate, or springform pan and cut into wedges. It looks and tastes so good that you'll be amazed that it's made with pantry ingredients.

1 (15.5-ounce) can chickpeas, drained and rinsed
1 (14-ounce) can artichoke hearts, drained
2 cups water or vegetable broth
1 cup couscous

1 tablespoon dehydrated minced onions
2 tablespoons nutritional yeast
2 teaspoons freshly squeezed lemon juice
Salt and freshly ground black pepper
½ cup chopped walnut pieces

Preheat the oven to 375°F. Lightly oil a springform pan or a pie plate.

In a food processor, combine the chickpeas and artichoke hearts and pulse to finely chop.

Bring the water to a boil in a saucepan. Stir in the couscous and onions, then stir in the chickpea and artichoke mixture. Remove from the heat and stir in the nutritional yeast, lemon juice, and salt and pepper to taste.

Press the mixture firmly and evenly into the springform pan and sprinkle the top with the walnuts. Bake for 12 minutes, then remove from the oven and let cool for 10 minutes before serving. This can also be served at room temperature, if you prefer.

antipasto tart

serves 4

You'll feel like a magician when you whip up this elegant, savory tart using on-hand ingredients. Made with puff pastry from your freezer (Pepperidge Farm brand is vegan) and several pantry ingredients, this flaky and flavorful dish can be cut into smaller servings as an appetizer or four large servings as a main dish. A tossed salad is a good accompaniment.

1 (10 by 14-inch) sheet frozen
   vegan puff pastry, thawed
1 (15.5-ounce) can white beans,
   drained and rinsed
1 tablespoon nutritional yeast
1 teaspoon dried basil
½ teaspoon dried oregano
½ teaspoon garlic powder
Salt and freshly ground black pepper

1 (8-ounce) can marinated artichoke
   hearts, drained and chopped
1 jarred roasted red bell pepper,
   cut into ½-inch dice
4 reconstituted or oil-packed
   sun-dried tomatoes, cut into thin strips
⅓ cup kalamata olives, pitted and halved
2 teaspoons capers, drained
2 tablespoons minced fresh
   Italian parsley

Preheat the oven to 400°F.

Roll out the puff pastry and press it into an 8 by 10-inch baking pan or fit it into a 10-inch tart pan.

In a food processor, combine the white beans, nutritional yeast, basil, oregano, garlic powder, and salt and pepper to taste. Process until smooth. Spread the white bean mixture on the top surface of the puff pastry, leaving a ½-inch border along the edge. Bake for 10 minutes.

While the pastry is baking, combine all of the remaining ingredients except the parsley in a medium bowl and toss to combine. Drain the antipasto mixture of any residual liquid and spread the mixture evenly on top of the baked pastry. Return to the oven and bake for another 15 minutes or until the pastry is nicely browned. Serve hot, sprinkled with the parsley.

pantry burgers

serves 4 to 6

These great-tasting burgers are a good reason to keep a small can of potatoes on hand, along with black beans and oats. They are easy, economical, and delicious, whether served in a bun with all the trimmings or topped with brown gravy (see page 173).

1 (15.5-ounce) can black beans,
    drained and rinsed
1 (8-ounce) can sliced white potatoes,
    drained and chopped (or 1 cup
    leftover chopped cooked potatoes)
½ teaspoon garlic powder

½ teaspoon smoked paprika
½ teaspoon salt
¼ teaspoon freshly ground black pepper
¾ cup old-fashioned rolled oats
2 tablespoons olive oil

Blot the beans and potatoes to remove any excess moisture.

In a food processor, combine the beans, potatoes, garlic powder, paprika, salt, and pepper. Pulse until finely chopped. Add the oats and pulse until well combined. Pinch the mixture to make sure it holds together well. If it is too moist, add more oats and process to incorporate.

Divide the mixture into 4 to 6 equal portions and use your hands to shape into burgers.

Heat the oil in a large skillet over medium heat. Cook the burgers until nicely browned on both sides, about 5 minutes per side. Serve hot as desired.

curried red bean and pumpkin soup

serves 4

This colorful soup made with pantry ingredients has an amazingly rich depth of flavor thanks to the curry powder and unsweetened coconut milk. If you have any fresh or frozen spinach on hand, it makes a great addition.

1 (15-ounce) can solid-pack pumpkin
1 tablespoon curry powder
1 teaspoon natural sugar
1 (15-ounce) can unsweetened
   coconut milk

1 to 2 cups vegetable broth
Salt and freshly ground black pepper
2 (15.5-ounce) cans dark red kidney
   beans, drained and rinsed
2 tablespoons pumpkin seeds (optional)

In a large saucepan, combine the pumpkin, curry powder, and sugar. Stir in the coconut milk until well blended. Stir in 1 cup of the vegetable broth, adding more if needed to achieve the desired consistency. Season with salt and pepper to taste. Stir in the kidney beans and simmer for 10 to 15 minutes to heat through and allow the flavors to develop, stirring occasionally. Taste to adjust the seasonings, if needed, and serve hot, sprinkled with the pumpkin seeds, if using.

pantry corn bread

serves 6 to 8

Creamed corn (instead of liquid) is combined with a box of corn bread mix for a quick and easy corn bread with extra corn flavor. The optional chipotle chiles add a nice kick. If you prefer not to use a boxed mix, use the dry ingredients listed in the recipe instead.

1 (13- to 16-ounce) box corn bread mix or:

DRY INGREDIENTS
2 cups yellow cornmeal
¼ cup unbleached all-purpose flour
2 teaspoons baking powder
½ teaspoon baking soda
½ teaspoon salt

2 (16-ounce) cans creamed corn
½ to 1 cup plain unsweetened almond milk or other nondairy milk
1 teaspoon freshly squeezed lemon juice
2 canned chipotle chiles in adobo, minced (optional)

Preheat the oven to 400°F. Lightly oil an 8-inch square baking pan.

Place the corn bread mix in a large bowl (or combine all of the dry ingredients). Add the creamed corn, ½ cup of the almond milk, lemon juice, and chiles, if using. Stir to mix well. Add as much of the remaining almond milk as needed if the batter is too dry.

Scrape the batter evenly into the prepared pan. Bake until a toothpick inserted in the center comes out clean, about 35 minutes. Let cool before cutting.

pantry pumpkin cake

serves 8 to 10

This quick-fix cake is perfect for impromptu dinner guests or just because. Variations abound: Add your choice of toasted chopped pecans or walnuts, dried cranberries, and/or vegan chocolate chips. A splash of rum will give it a grown-up taste. Serve as is, dust with confectioners' sugar (after it's cool), or whip up your favorite frosting, if you've got the ingredients on hand.

1 box vegan spice cake mix
1 cup canned solid-pack pumpkin
1½ teaspoons pumpkin pie spice
¼ cup natural sugar or pure maple syrup
½ cup unsweetened almond milk
    or other nondairy milk

½ cup chopped toasted pecans
    or walnuts (optional)
½ cup vegan chocolate chips (optional)
½ cup dried sweetened
    cranberries (optional)

Preheat the oven to 350°F. Lightly oil a 10-inch square baking pan.

In a large bowl, combine the spice cake mix with the pumpkin, pumpkin pie spice, sugar, and almond milk. Stir to mix well. Add the pecans, chocolate chips, and cranberries, if using, folding them into the batter. Scrape the batter evenly into the prepared pan. Bake until a toothpick inserted in the center comes out clean, about 30 minutes. Let cool before adding any additional toppings (see headnote). Cut and serve.

pantry black forest cake

serves 8

When you're in the mood for a decadent dessert but don't have the time or energy to make a from-scratch cake, you'll be glad you have these ingredients in your pantry. One bowl and no measuring mean no messy cleanup. Just mix, bake, and enjoy. If you happen to have kirsch on hand, a generous splash lends authenticity (and flavor) to the cake. This is delicious and moist as is, but if you want to fancy it up, spread some additional cherry pie filling (or a thin layer of cherry preserves) on top of the cake and sprinkle with some chocolate curls when ready to serve.

1 box vegan chocolate cake mix
1 (21-ounce) can cherry pie filling
3 tablespoons kirsch or water

Preheat the oven to 350°F. Lightly oil a 9-inch baking pan.

In a large bowl, combine the cake mix, pie filling, and kirsch. Stir to mix well. Scrape the batter evenly into the prepared pan. Bake until a toothpick inserted in the center comes out clean, 35 to 40 minutes. Let cool before cutting.

from
the oven

The recipes in this chapter differ from those in the rest of this book in one significant way. While they take only 30 minutes or less of "active time" to prepare, they also require additional time in the oven.

At first glance, this may not seem like "quick-fix" to you, but I believe that they are in some ways even more convenient than many stovetop recipes. For one thing, they can be assembled ahead of time, allowing you to prepare the recipe in advance and then pop the dish in the oven when needed. That can come in handy when you know you'll be coming home late or when company's coming. Just heat and serve.

The recipes range from casual fare such as Migas-Inspired Frittata (page 168), White Pizza with Artichoke-Arugula Pesto (page 171), and Mac and Queso Salsa (page 174) to company-worthy dishes such as Mediterranean Vegetable Strudel (page 167), Falafel-Stuffed Portobellos with Tahini Sauce (page 163), and Blushing Baked Ziti (page 162). I hope you enjoy this selection of satisfying and delicious recipes from the oven as much as I do.

pretzel-topped mustard
mac uncheese

serves 4

The unique flavor of this comfort food casserole, topped with crunchy pretzel crumbs, calls to mind the delicious combination of a warm, soft pretzel topped with mustard. If you assemble it ahead of time, it can go from oven to table in about 30 minutes.

8 ounces elbow macaroni
1 tablespoon olive oil or ¼ cup water
1 small yellow onion, chopped
2 cloves garlic, minced
1 cup broken pretzels
⅔ cup raw cashews, soaked in
   water for 3 hours or overnight
2 cups vegetable broth,
   or more if needed

1 cup home-cooked or
   canned white beans
⅓ cup nutritional yeast
2 tablespoons freshly
   squeezed lemon juice
1 tablespoon yellow mustard,
   or more if needed
½ teaspoon salt
¼ teaspoon freshly ground black pepper

Preheat the oven to 350°F. Lightly oil a 2-quart baking dish or spray it with nonstick cooking spray.

Cook the macaroni in a pot of boiling salted water until it is al dente. Drain well and return to the pot. Set aside.

Heat the oil in a small skillet over medium heat. Add the onion and cook until softened, about 5 minutes. Add the garlic and cook for 1 minute longer. Set aside.

Pulse the pretzels in a food processor to make fine crumbs. Transfer to a bowl and set aside. Do not wash out the food processor for the next step, if using.

Drain the cashews. In a food processor or high-speed blender, combine the cashews and broth and blend until smooth. Transfer the onion mixture to the food processor with the cashew mixture. Add the white beans, nutritional yeast, lemon juice, mustard, salt, and pepper. Process to blend well. Taste and adjust the seasonings, adding more salt or mustard, if needed.

Add the sauce to the pot with the cooked pasta, stirring to coat. Transfer the mixture to the prepared baking dish. Sprinkle the top of the casserole with the pretzel crumbs. Cover tightly and bake for 25 minutes or until hot. Uncover and bake for 7 to 9 minutes longer to brown the topping.

blushing baked ziti

serves 4 to 6

This satisfying casserole is loaded with protein thanks to the inclusion of both tofu and white beans. It makes a great weeknight supper because it can be assembled ahead of time and then baked when needed. While it bakes, you can put together a nice green salad to go with it, set the table, and maybe pour some wine. Before you know it, dinner is served.

8 ounces ridged ziti
1 tablespoon olive oil
3 cloves garlic, minced
1 teaspoon dried basil
½ teaspoon dried oregano
½ cup nutritional yeast
¼ cup vegetable broth or dry red wine
1 teaspoon salt
½ teaspoon freshly ground black pepper

2½ cups marinara sauce
¾ cup plain unsweetened almond
  milk or other nondairy milk
12 ounces extra-firm tofu, drained,
  pressed, and crumbled
2 tablespoons freshly
  squeezed lemon juice
⅓ cup shredded vegan cheese (optional)

Cook the ziti in a large pot of boiling salted water until it is al dente. Drain and return to the pot. Set aside. Preheat the oven to 350°F. Lightly grease a 9-inch baking dish.

Heat the oil in a small saucepan over medium heat. Add the garlic, basil, and oregano and cook, stirring until fragrant, about 30 seconds. Stir in the nutritional yeast, then stir in the broth and cook, stirring to blend. Add ½ teaspoon of the salt and ¼ teaspoon of the pepper, then stir in the marinara sauce and ½ cup of the almond milk. Simmer for 5 minutes, then turn off the heat and set the sauce aside.

In a bowl, combine the crumbled tofu, lemon juice, the remaining ½ teaspoon salt, and the remaining ¼ teaspoon pepper. Add the remaining ¼ cup almond milk and mix well, mashing to incorporate the ingredients.

Add the tofu mixture to the cooked, drained ziti, along with 1½ cups of the sauce. Stir to mix well, then transfer the pasta mixture evenly into the prepared baking dish. Pour the remaining sauce over the pasta and bake for 30 minutes. Sprinkle the cheese, if using, over the top during the last 10 minutes of baking time to give it time to melt. Let cool for 10 minutes before serving.

falafel-stuffed portobellos
with tahini sauce

serves 4

A creamy tahini sauce cloaks these falafel-stuffed mushrooms for an easy and elegant dinner entrée that falafel fans will love. For a delicious variation, use bell peppers instead of mushrooms.

MUSHROOMS AND STUFFING
4 large portobello mushroom caps,
   stems and gills removed
1½ cups home-cooked chickpeas, or
   1 (15.5-ounce) can, drained and rinsed
2 tablespoons tahini
2 tablespoons minced yellow onion
1 clove garlic, minced
2 tablespoons chopped
   fresh Italian parsley
1 tablespoon tamari soy sauce
1 teaspoon freshly squeezed lemon juice
1 teaspoon ground cumin

1 teaspoon ground coriander
Salt and freshly ground black pepper
¼ cup panko bread crumbs,
   or more if needed

SAUCE
¾ cup tahini
3 tablespoons freshly
   squeezed lemon juice
1 tablespoon tamari soy sauce
2 small cloves garlic, minced
¼ teaspoon salt
½ cup water, or more if needed

To make the mushrooms: Preheat the oven to 400°F and lightly oil a large baking dish. Arrange the mushroom caps, stemmed side down, in the baking dish and bake for 10 minutes to soften.

While the mushrooms are baking, make the stuffing: In a food processor, combine the chickpeas, tahini, onion, garlic, parsley, tamari, and lemon juice. Add the cumin, coriander, and salt and pepper to taste and pulse to combine. Add the bread crumbs and pulse to combine while retaining some texture in the chickpeas.

Flip over the baked mushrooms and spoon the stuffing mixture into the mushroom caps, sprinkling additional crumbs on top, if desired. Bake for about 20 minutes or until the mushrooms are tender and the stuffing is hot.

While the stuffed mushrooms are baking, make the sauce: In a bowl, combine the tahini, lemon juice, tamari, garlic, and salt. Stir to combine. Add the water a little at a time as needed to make a smooth, creamy sauce, adding additional water if needed. Taste and adjust the seasonings, if needed. Serve the mushrooms hot with the sauce spooned over the top.

bajan macaroni pie

serves 4

Inspired by the traditional dish of Barbados, this unusual take on mac and cheese is made with mustard and vegan mayo and your choice of Cheesy Sauce (page 133) or shredded vegan cheddar. The inclusion of bell pepper, scallions, and tomato make it colorful as well as delicious.

8 ounces penne
1 tablespoon olive oil
1 medium yellow onion, minced
1 red or green bell pepper,
  seeded and minced
1 clove garlic, minced
4 scallions, chopped
2 teaspoons smoked paprika
½ teaspoon dried thyme
¼ teaspoon cayenne
⅛ teaspoon ground cloves (optional)
¼ cup vegan mayonnaise
2 tablespoons yellow mustard

2 tablespoons nutritional yeast
1 tablespoon freshly
  squeezed lemon juice
1 cup plain unsweetened almond
  milk or other nondairy milk
⅓ cup chopped fresh Italian parsley
1 teaspoon salt
1 teaspoon freshly ground black pepper
½ cup shredded vegan cheddar
  cheese (optional)
1 large fresh tomato, thinly sliced
¼ cup fine dried bread crumbs

Preheat the oven to 350°F and lightly oil a 2-quart baking dish. Cook the pasta in a pot of boiling salted water until it is al dente. Do not overcook. Drain well and return to the pot.

While the pasta is cooking, heat the oil in a medium skillet over medium heat. Add the onion, bell pepper, garlic, and scallions and cook until softened, about 5 minutes. Stir in the paprika, thyme, cayenne, and cloves, if using, then scrape the cooked vegetable mixture into the pot containing the cooked, drained pasta.

In a separate bowl, combine the mayonnaise, mustard, nutritional yeast, lemon juice, almond milk, parsley, salt, and pepper. Stir in ¼ cup of the cheese, if using, and mix well, then add to the pasta mixture, stirring to combine. Transfer the macaroni mixture to the baking dish, spreading evenly. Arrange the tomato slices on top of the macaroni. Sprinkle the top with the bread crumbs and the remaining ¼ cup cheese. Bake for 30 to 35 minutes, until hot and the top is golden brown.

roasted brussels sprouts and chickpeas

serves 4

Turn the oven on to preheat before you begin your prep, and you can have this yummy combo on the table in 30 minutes. I adore roasted Brussels sprouts (it's the only way I prepare them), and I also love roasted chickpeas. Together they make a wonderful main dish that can be served as is, with a squeeze of lemon, or topped with the Cheesy Sauce on page 133. This recipe serves four as a side dish or two as a main dish. If you want to bulk it up, roast some thinly sliced potatoes or sweet potatoes along with the Brussels sprouts, or serve over rice or quinoa.

1 pound Brussels sprouts,
**   trimmed and quartered**
1½ cups home-cooked chickpeas,
**   or 1 (15.5-ounce) can, drained,**
**   rinsed, and blotted dry**

2 tablespoons olive oil
1 tablespoon nutritional yeast
½ teaspoon smoked paprika
½ teaspoon salt
¼ teaspoon freshly ground black pepper

Preheat the oven to 400°F. Lightly oil a baking sheet. Spread the Brussels sprouts in a single layer on the baking sheet. Bake for 10 minutes. Remove from the oven, add the chickpeas, and stir to combine. Return to the oven and bake for 5 to 10 minutes longer, or until the Brussels sprouts are lightly browned and crispy and the chickpeas are hot.

Transfer to a bowl and drizzle on the olive oil. Sprinkle with the nutritional yeast, paprika, salt, and pepper and toss to combine. Serve hot.

red bean loaf with barbecue glaze

serves 4 to 6

This hearty loaf comes together quickly and can be assembled in advance. If you're a fan of barbecue sauce, you might want to double (or triple) the amount of glaze to slather on your slices of bean loaf at the table.

1 tablespoon olive oil or ¼ cup water
1 small yellow onion, minced
2 cloves garlic, minced
1 tablespoon dried thyme
3 cups cooked dark red kidney beans, or 2 (15.5-ounce) cans, well drained, rinsed, and blotted dry
¾ cup ketchup
2 tablespoons vegan Worcestershire sauce or tamari soy sauce

1 tablespoon Dijon mustard
¾ cup quick-cooking oats
½ cup ground walnuts
½ cup vital wheat gluten flour
2 tablespoons minced fresh Italian parsley
Salt and freshly ground black pepper
2 tablespoons cider vinegar
2 to 3 teaspoons natural sugar
1 tablespoon yellow mustard

Preheat the oven to 350°F. Lightly oil a large loaf pan or 1½-quart baking dish.

Heat the oil in a small skillet over medium-high heat. Add the onion and cook for 5 minutes to soften. Add the garlic and thyme and cook for 1 minute longer. Set aside.

Place the kidney beans in a large bowl and mash well. Add ½ cup of the ketchup, the Worcestershire sauce, Dijon mustard, and the reserved onion mixture and mix until well combined. Add the oats, walnuts, vital wheat gluten flour, and parsley. Season with about 1 teaspoon salt and ¼ teaspoon pepper. Stir well to mix thoroughly. Transfer the mixture to the prepared pan and press to make sure the loaf holds together and is evenly distributed in the pan.

In a small bowl, combine the remaining ¼ cup ketchup with the vinegar, sugar, and yellow mustard and mix well. Spread the mixture on top of the loaf. Cover and bake for 50 minutes, then uncover and continue baking until lightly browned and firm, about 10 minutes longer. Remove from the oven and let cool for 10 minutes before slicing.

mediterranean vegetable strudel

serves 4

Flaky pastry outside and a flavor-packed filling inside make this strudel a win-win! Keep a box of puff pastry in the freezer (Pepperidge Farm brand is vegan) for an easy way to transform everyday ingredients into company fare.

1 tablespoon olive oil, plus more
   for brushing (optional)
1 small red onion, chopped
1 medium zucchini, trimmed and chopped
6 ounces cremini mushrooms, chopped
3 cloves garlic, minced
1 (6-ounce) jar marinated artichoke
   hearts, drained and chopped
1 roasted red bell pepper, chopped
3 tablespoons fresh basil leaves, chopped
1 teaspoon dried marjoram
½ teaspoon salt
¼ teaspoon freshly ground black pepper

1 (10 by 14-inch) sheet frozen
   vegan puff pastry, thawed
1½ cups home-cooked cannellini
   beans, or 1 (15.5-ounce) can,
   drained and rinsed
1 tablespoon white wine vinegar or
   freshly squeezed lemon juice
2 teaspoons capers
2 tablespoons chopped
   fresh Italian parsley
2 tablespoons nutritional yeast
¼ cup ground walnuts, plus
   more for garnish

Preheat the oven to 400°F and line a baking sheet with parchment paper.

Heat the oil in a large skillet over medium-high heat. Add the onion, zucchini, mushrooms, and garlic. Cook, stirring, until softened, about 5 minutes. Add the artichokes, roasted bell pepper, basil, marjoram, salt, and pepper. Stir to mix well, then remove from the heat to cool.

Roll out the pastry sheet on a lightly floured work surface until it is very thin and about an inch or two larger all around.

In a bowl, mash the white beans, vinegar, and capers. Stir in the parsley and nutritional yeast and mix well to combine. Spread the bean mixture across the surface of the rolled-out dough. Drain any liquid from the reserved vegetables, then spread the vegetable mixture evenly over the bean mixture. Sprinkle the vegetables with the walnuts. Grasp the dough on one edge and roll up the dough to enclose the filling. Pinch the ends and the seam to seal it. Arrange the strudel on the baking sheet. If desired, brush the top lightly with olive oil and sprinkle with more walnuts.

Bake until the strudel crust is nicely browned, about 20 minutes. Let sit for 10 minutes before slicing crosswise with a serrated knife to serve.

migas-inspired frittata

serves 4

The vegan migas I make with tofu and strips of corn tortillas reminds me of a tofu scramble, so it made sense that it would transform into a delicious frittata—and it does! You can make it hot or mild according to your own taste.

1 pound firm tofu, well
   drained and pressed
¾ cup vegetable broth
2 tablespoons dry white wine
1 tablespoon freshly
   squeezed lemon juice
¼ cup nutritional yeast
1 tablespoon cornstarch or tapioca starch
1 teaspoon garlic powder
½ teaspoon salt
¼ teaspoon ground black pepper
⅓ cup tomato salsa, plus more for serving

1 tablespoon olive oil or
   3 tablespoons water
1 small yellow onion, minced
2 cloves garlic, minced
2 scallions, minced
4 (6-inch) corn tortillas, torn
   into bite-size pieces
1 (4-ounce) can chopped green
   chiles, drained (hot or mild)
1 medium fresh tomato, chopped
1 tablespoon minced fresh cilantro
Hot sauce, for serving

Preheat the oven to 375°F and lightly oil a 9- or 10-inch deep-dish pie plate or round or oval shallow baking dish. In a food processor or blender, combine the tofu, broth, wine, lemon juice, nutritional yeast, cornstarch, garlic powder, salt, and pepper. Add the salsa and process until smooth and well blended.

Heat the oil in a large skillet over medium heat. Add the onion and cook until softened, 5 minutes. Add the garlic, scallions, and tortilla pieces and cook for 2 minutes. Stir in the chiles and the tofu mixture and cook, stirring, until hot and well combined. Add the chopped tomato and cilantro and stir to combine. Taste and adjust the seasonings, if needed.

Spread the cooked vegetable mixture evenly in the bottom of the baking dish. Bake until firm, golden brown, and slightly puffed up, about 40 minutes. Cut into wedges and serve hot topped with hot sauce, and additional salsa on the side.

three-tomato pizza

makes 1 (12-inch) pizza

Pizza can be a quick and easy dinner when you keep pizza dough on hand. Whether you make the dough yourself or buy it ready-made, keep a stash in the freezer. Just remember to bring your dough to room temperature before using.

Dough for 1 (12-inch) pizza, homemade (page 16) or store bought, at room temperature
½ cup tomato sauce
½ teaspoon dried oregano
½ cup cooked white beans or crumbled tofu
2 cloves garlic, crushed
2 tablespoons nutritional yeast

2 tablespoons reconstituted or oil-packed sun-dried tomatoes, chopped
1 teaspoon dried basil
½ teaspoon salt
¼ teaspoon freshly ground black pepper
¼ teaspoon red pepper flakes
2 plum tomatoes, cut into thin slices
3 tablespoons kalamata olives, pitted and chopped
½ cup crushed pine nuts

Place the oven rack in the bottom position of the oven. Preheat the oven to 450°F.

Stretch the dough into a 12-inch round on a baking sheet or pizza stone. Use your fingertips to form a rim around the perimeter of the crust.

Spread the tomato sauce evenly on top of the pizza dough, to within ½ inch of the edge. Sprinkle with the oregano.

In a food processor, combine the white beans, garlic, nutritional yeast, sun-dried tomatoes, basil, salt, pepper, and red pepper flakes. Process until smooth. Spoon the mixture on top of the tomato sauce and spread with the back of a spoon. Arrange the plum tomato slices on top of the pizza and sprinkle with the olives and pine nuts.

Bake until the crust is golden brown, about 15 minutes. Serve hot.

white pizza with artichoke-arugula pesto

makes 1 (12-inch) pizza

If you make your toppings ahead of time and have your dough at room temperature, this pizza can be assembled and baked in just minutes.

Dough for 1 (12-inch) pizza,
   homemade (page 16) or store
   bought, at room temperature
1½ cups home-cooked white beans, or
   1 (15.5-ounce) can, drained and rinsed
3 cloves garlic, crushed
2 tablespoons water
2 tablespoons freshly
   squeezed lemon juice

3 tablespoons nutritional yeast
½ teaspoon dried basil
½ teaspoon dried oregano
Salt and freshly ground black pepper
2 cups coarsely chopped arugula
½ cup fresh basil leaves
⅓ cup almonds or walnuts
1 (6-ounce) jar marinated artichoke
   hearts, well drained

Place the oven rack in the bottom position of the oven. Preheat the oven to 450°F.

Stretch the dough into a 12-inch round onto a baking sheet or pizza stone. Use your fingertips to form a rim around the perimeter of the crust. Bake the crust for 10 minutes, then remove from the oven.

In a food processor, combine the white beans and garlic and process to a paste. Add the water, lemon juice, nutritional yeast, basil, oregano, and salt and pepper to taste. Blend until smooth. Spread the mixture evenly on top of the partially baked pizza crust to within ½ inch of the edge.

In the same food processor, combine the arugula, basil, and almonds and process to a paste. Add the artichokes and about ½ teaspoon of salt, and process until smooth. The pesto should be thick. Drop the pesto, by the spoonful, onto the white bean topping. Bake the pizza for an additional 10 minutes, or until the crust is nicely browned. Serve hot.

scottish oat loaf

serves 4

Oats and Scotch are about the only things this loaf has in common with haggis, but it's a tasty and animal-friendly way to celebrate Robert Burns Day on January 25. Serve with the traditional neeps (turnips) and tatties (potatoes) and Go-To Brown Gravy (recipe follows).

1 tablespoon olive oil or ¼ cup water
1 large yellow onion, minced
1 large carrot, finely shredded
4 ounces white mushrooms, finely chopped
1½ cups old-fashioned rolled oats
1½ cups home-cooked kidney beans, or 1 (15.5-ounce) can, drained, rinsed, and blotted dry
⅔ cup ground walnuts

⅓ cup vital wheat gluten flour
2 tablespoons minced fresh Italian parsley
2 tablespoons Scotch whisky
1½ tablespoons tamari soy sauce
1½ teaspoons dried thyme
⅛ teaspoon ground nutmeg
⅛ teaspoon cayenne
Salt and freshly ground black pepper

Preheat the oven to 350°F. Lightly oil a 5 by 9-inch loaf pan.

Heat the oil in a large saucepan over medium-high heat. Add the onion and carrot and cook for 5 minutes to soften. Add the mushrooms and cook for a minute or two to soften. Stir in the oats and decrease the heat to low. Cook, stirring occasionally, for 3 to 5 minutes or until all the liquid is cooked out.

Mash the kidney beans well, then stir them into the oat mixture. Add the walnuts, vital wheat gluten flour, parsley, whisky, tamari, thyme, nutmeg, cayenne, and salt and black pepper to taste. Mix well to combine.

Spoon the stuffing mixture into the prepared loaf pan and press the mixture evenly into the pan, smoothing the top. Cover and bake for 45 minutes. Uncover and bake for another 15 minutes longer or until firm. Remove from the oven and let cool for 10 minutes before slicing.

go-to brown gravy
makes about 1¾ cups

I call this "go-to" gravy for obvious reasons—it's the one I go to most often when I want a quick and easy but flavorful gravy to top burgers, patties, seitan, grains, and loaves such as the Scottish Oat Loaf. For a creamier gravy, use the optional almond milk (or other plain unsweetened nondairy milk) instead of the remaining broth.

1 tablespoon olive oil
⅓ cup minced yellow onion
1 clove garlic, minced
1 teaspoon minced fresh thyme
    or ½ teaspoon dried
3 tablespoons unbleached
    all-purpose flour
1½ cups vegetable broth (as needed)
2 tablespoons tamari soy sauce
1 teaspoon browning sauce (try
    Kitchen Bouquet or Gravy Master)
⅓ cup plain unsweetened almond milk
    or other nondairy milk (optional)
Salt and freshly ground black pepper

Heat the oil in a saucepan over medium heat. Add the onion and garlic and cook until soft, 5 minutes. Sprinkle on the thyme and flour and stir to mix well. Slowly stir in 1 cup of the broth and continue stirring until it thickens and becomes smooth. Decrease the heat to low and stir in the tamari and browning sauce, and then the almond milk or as much of the remaining ½ cup broth as desired. Season with salt and pepper to taste. For a smoother texture, puree the gravy in a blender or food processor, or use an immersion blender to puree it right in the pot. Serve hot. Store leftovers in a tightly sealed container in the refrigerator for up to 5 days.

mac and queso salsa

serves 4 to 6

I love the way the flavors come together in this hearty casserole. The white beans add protein and creaminess to the sauce, while the tortilla chip topping adds crunch. Use your favorite brand of salsa—hot or mild—according to your preference. The avocado and olives added at the end aren't required, but I do recommend them.

8 ounces elbow macaroni
1½ cups home-cooked navy beans or
    other white beans, or 1 (15.5-ounce)
    can, drained, rinsed, and blotted dry
2 cups tomato salsa
¼ cup nutritional yeast
2 tablespoons freshly
    squeezed lemon juice
½ teaspoon garlic powder
½ teaspoon onion powder
½ teaspoon smoked paprika
½ teaspoon salt

¼ teaspoon freshly ground black pepper
½ to 1 cup plain unsweetened almond
    milk or other nondairy milk or
    vegetable broth, as needed
½ cup finely crushed tortilla
    chips or corn chips
1 Hass avocado (optional)
¼ cup black olives, pitted and
    chopped (optional)
2 tablespoons chopped fresh
    cilantro (optional)

Preheat the oven to 350°F. Lightly oil a 2-quart baking dish or spray it with nonstick cooking spray.

Cook the macaroni in a pot of boiling salted water until it is al dente. Drain and return to the pot. Set aside.

In a blender or food processor, combine the beans, salsa, nutritional yeast, lemon juice, garlic powder, onion powder, paprika, salt, and pepper. Process until well blended, then add as much of the almond milk as needed to make a smooth sauce and process until very smooth. Taste and adjust the seasonings, if needed.

Add the sauce to the pasta and mix well. Transfer to the prepared baking dish and spread evenly. Sprinkle the top with the crushed tortilla chips. Cover and bake for 20 minutes or until hot. Uncover and bake for 10 minutes longer to crisp the topping.

Halve and pit the avocado, if using. Scoop out the flesh with a spoon and dice. Serve hot topped with the avocado, olives, and cilantro, if using.

white bean and butternut scalloped potatoes

serves 4 to 6

With white beans in the creamy sauce and layers of butternut squash alongside the potatoes, this scalloped potato casserole tastes decadent. Serve with a crisp green salad for a satisfying meal.

1 tablespoon olive oil
1 small yellow onion, chopped
3 cloves garlic, minced
½ teaspoon dried thyme
1½ cups home-cooked white beans, or
    1 (15.5-ounce) can, drained and rinsed
½ cup vegan cream cheese
2 tablespoons cornstarch
    or potato starch

1 cup plain unsweetened almond
    milk or other nondairy milk
1 teaspoon Dijon mustard
Salt and freshly ground black pepper
½ to 1 cup vegetable broth (as needed)
1½ pounds russet potatoes, peeled
    and cut into ⅛-inch-thick slices
1 pound butternut squash, peeled
    and cut into ¼-inch-thick slices

Preheat the oven to 375°F. Lightly oil a large shallow baking dish.

Heat the oil in a small skillet over medium heat. Add the onion, garlic, and thyme and cook for about 4 minutes to soften. Transfer the onion mixture to a high-speed blender or food processor. Add the beans, cream cheese, cornstarch, almond milk, mustard, and salt and pepper to taste. Add as much of the broth as needed to make a smooth sauce and process until smooth and creamy.

Spread a thin layer of the sauce in the bottom of the prepared baking dish. Spread a layer of potatoes over the sauce, followed by a layer of squash. Season with salt and pepper to taste. Top with a layer of sauce, and continue layering until all of the potatoes, squash, and sauce are used, ending with a layer of sauce. Cover tightly and bake until the vegetables are tender, about 50 minutes. Uncover and continue baking for another 10 to 15 minutes to lightly brown the top.

mediterranean polenta pie

serves 4

Artichoke hearts, tomato slices, bell pepper, and olives top this savory pie seasoned with basil and oregano. If you can find instant or quick-cooking polenta, you can decrease the preparation time significantly.

3¼ cups water
Salt
1 cup medium-grind yellow cornmeal
3 scallions, finely minced
1 teaspoon dried basil
½ teaspoon dried oregano
Freshly ground black pepper

4 marinated artichoke
hearts, thinly sliced
2 plum tomatoes, thinly sliced
⅓ cup kalamata olives,
pitted and chopped
1 roasted red bell pepper, chopped
½ cup shredded vegan cheddar
cheese (optional)

Preheat the oven to 375°F. Lightly oil a shallow 10-inch square baking dish or round pie pan.

Bring the water to a boil in a large saucepan over high heat. Lower the heat to medium, add 1 teaspoon salt, and slowly whisk in the cornmeal, stirring constantly. Decrease the heat to low and continue to cook, stirring frequently, until thick, about 20 minutes. Stir in the scallions, basil, and oregano, and season with salt and pepper to taste. Spoon the polenta into the prepared pan and spread it evenly.

Arrange the artichoke and tomato slices on top of the polenta. Season with salt and pepper to taste and sprinkle evenly with the olives and bell pepper. Sprinkle with the cheese, if using. Cover and bake for 15 minutes, then uncover and continue baking for 10 minutes longer to lightly brown the top. Serve hot.

black bean–quinoa loaf

serves 4

This protein-packed loaf is a great way to use leftover quinoa. Serve with your favorite sauce or gravy, such as Go-To Brown Gravy (page 173).

1 tablespoon olive oil
1 medium yellow onion, minced
2 cloves garlic, minced
1 tablespoon dried thyme
1½ cups home-cooked black beans, or 1 (15.5-ounce) can, drained and rinsed
2 cups cooked quinoa
⅓ cup tomato sauce, barbecue sauce, or ketchup
2 tablespoons tamari soy sauce
½ cup quick-cooking oats
½ cup vital wheat gluten flour
½ cup ground walnuts
2 tablespoons minced fresh Italian parsley
½ teaspoon salt
¼ teaspoon freshly ground black pepper

Preheat the oven to 350°F. Lightly oil a 5 by 9-inch loaf pan.

Heat the oil in a medium skillet over medium-high heat. Add the onion and sauté for 5 minutes to soften. Add the garlic and thyme and cook for 1 minute longer.

In a food processor, combine the black beans, quinoa, tomato sauce, tamari, and the reserved onion mixture and process to mix well.

In a large bowl, combine the oats, vital wheat gluten flour, walnuts, parsley, salt, and pepper. Add the bean mixture and stir well to mix thoroughly.

Transfer the mixture to the prepared pan and press to make sure the loaf holds together and is evenly distributed in the pan. Cover and bake for 45 minutes. Uncover and allow the loaf to cool for about 10 minutes before serving. Slice carefully with a serrated knife.

chapter 9

quick-fix desserts

When you read through the decadent-sounding recipe titles in this chapter, such as Baklava Palmiers (page 188), Pumpkin Brownies (page 197), and Raspberry Zabaglione (page 189), it may be hard to believe that these desserts can be ready to eat in 30 minutes or less, but it's true.

Some of them, such as Chocolate Chip–Cherry Ice Cream (page 200) and Peanut Butter and Banana Ice Cream (page 198), can benefit from a little time in the freezer. Others, such as Peach Melba Crisp (page 193) and Cherry-Chocolate Pie Balls (page 185), may be best after a little cooling time. But any way you slice it (or scoop, lick, or nibble it!), in 30 minutes or less, you've got dessert!

piña colada balls

These balls aren't too sweet as is, but be sure to use unsweetened coconut or they may become too sweet. If you don't want to use confectioners' sugar, then substitute 2 to 3 tablespoons of sweetened coconut for part of the unsweetened coconut and omit the confectioners' sugar. If you don't have dark rum, you can use ½ to 1 teaspoon rum extract and make up the rest of the liquid (to equal the 1 tablespoon) with pineapple juice or a little water or nondairy milk. Also, be sure you use dried pineapple pieces (not fresh or canned—they will be too wet!).

1 cup dried pineapple pieces
½ cup raw cashews or slivered almonds
½ cup old-fashioned rolled oats

½ cup unsweetened shredded
**   coconut, plus more to coat**
1 tablespoon confectioners' sugar
1 tablespoon Myers's dark rum

Combine all of the ingredients (except the additional coconut for coating) in a food processor and pulse to chop. Then process until finely chopped and well combined. The mixture should hold together easily. Roll the mixture into 1-inch balls. Roll the balls in the additional unsweetened shredded coconut to coat.

Arrange the balls on a plate to serve. They can be eaten right away but taste even better if allowed to sit at room temperature for a few hours to let the flavors meld.

date-pecan bars

makes 9 bars

Moist, chewy, and delicious, these tasty treats take just a few minutes to put together, and they bake up in 20 minutes. They make a great no-added-sugar after-school snack for kids or an anytime snack for you.

2 cups chopped pitted dates (soaked and drained, if your dates are dry)
1 cup chopped pecans
1 cup old-fashioned rolled oats
½ cup raisins
⅓ cup pure maple syrup

2 tablespoons almond butter
2 tablespoons vegan butter, melted
1 teaspoon vanilla extract
¾ teaspoon ground cinnamon
Pinch of ground nutmeg

Preheat the oven to 375°F. Lightly oil an 8-inch square baking pan.

In a food processor, combine the dates, pecans, oats, and raisins and process until crumbly. Add all of the remaining ingredients and process until well combined, adding a little water, a tablespoon at a time, if the mixture is too dry.

Press the mixture evenly into the prepared pan. Bake for 20 minutes, or until lightly browned. Let cool before cutting into bars to serve.

happy oatmeal cookies

makes 24 cookies

Perfectly soft and chewy, these cookies got their name because they can't help but make you happy when you eat one . . . or five. The nuts, chocolate chips, and dried fruit are optional, but I strongly suggest you include them if you want to be really happy.

1 cup white whole wheat flour (or
   your favorite flour for baking)
¾ cup natural sugar
1 teaspoon baking soda
1 teaspoon ground cinnamon
½ teaspoon salt
½ cup pure maple syrup
¼ cup neutral vegetable oil

¼ cup water
1½ teaspoons vanilla extract
1¾ cups old-fashioned rolled oats
⅓ cup raisins or dried
   cranberries (optional)
⅓ cup chopped toasted walnuts
   or pecans (optional)
⅓ cup vegan chocolate chips (optional)

Preheat the oven to 350°F. Lightly grease one or two baking sheets or line them with parchment paper.

In a large bowl, combine the flour, sugar, baking soda, cinnamon, and salt.

In a small bowl, combine the maple syrup, oil, water, and vanilla and mix well. Combine the wet ingredients with the dry ingredients, stirring to mix. Stir in the oats, then stir in the cranberries, walnuts, and chocolate chips, if using.

Drop the dough by the heaping tablespoonful about 1½ inches apart onto the prepared baking sheet. Flatten the cookies with your fingers or the back of a spoon. Bake for 12 minutes or until lightly browned on the bottom. Let cool on a rack for a few minutes. Cool completely before storing.

apricot-chocolate truffles

makes about 24 truffles

Not only are these rich, decadent truffles easy to make but they're also extremely versatile. You can change up the flavors by using different nuts and nut butters and/or other varieties of dried fruit and jam.

½ cup chopped dried apricots
½ cup roasted cashews,
   peanuts, or almonds
2 tablespoons apricot jam
1 tablespoon almond butter
½ cup high-quality unsweetened
   cocoa powder

1 cup confectioners' sugar
1 to 2 tablespoons plain unsweetened
   almond milk or other nondairy milk
Crushed toasted cashews, peanuts,
   or almonds, or unsweetened
   cocoa powder, for coating

Combine the apricots and cashews in a food processor and process until finely chopped. Add the jam and almond butter and process to combine. Add the cocoa powder and confectioners' sugar and pulse until well combined. Pinch some of the mixture between your fingers to see if it holds together. If not, add just enough of the almond milk until the mixture can be shaped into balls. If the truffle mixture is too soft to handle right after mixing, place the mixture in the refrigerator for a few minutes to firm up.

Shape a small amount of the mixture into a ball, rolling with your hands into a 1-inch ball. Repeat until the mixture is used up. Arrange the coatings of your choice on shallow plates. Roll the truffles in the coating to cover completely. Transfer to a plate and refrigerate until firm.

cherry-chocolate pie balls

makes 18 pie balls

To make short work of pitting cherries, consider buying a cherry pitter. You can also use it for olives. It works great and is fun to use. One 10 by 14-inch sheet of puff pastry will make about 18 pie balls—a single piecrust may make a few less. You can make as many or as few of them at a time as you wish (use 1 cherry and 3 chocolate chips per ball). These treats taste best when eaten fresh out of the oven, after cooling for just a few minutes.

1 (10 by 14-inch) sheet frozen
   Pepperidge Farm Puff Pastry or
   1 (10-inch) single piecrust, thawed
18 fresh cherries, pitted and blotted dry
54 semisweet vegan chocolate chips

Preheat the oven to 400°F. Line a baking sheet with parchment paper.

Unfold the sheet of puff pastry. Cut the pastry along the folds to make 3 strips. On a flat surface, cut each strip into 6 equal pieces. If using pie dough, roll it out thinly and then cut it into 3-inch square pieces.

Carefully stuff each cherry with 3 chocolate chips. Wrap one piece of pastry around each stuffed cherry, carefully pinching any seams closed to seal the cherry inside the pastry. Gently roll each ball between your hands to smooth it. Place the balls on the prepared baking sheet, about 1 inch apart.

Bake until nicely browned, about 20 minutes. Let cool on a rack for a few minutes. These are best served while still warm.

berry fool-ish

serves 4

Reminiscent of the old English fruit pudding known as "fool" that's made with whipped cream, this "fool-ish" dessert is made with cashews and tofu for a healthier but still delicious treat.

¾ cup raw cashews, soaked in
    water for 3 hours or overnight
1 cup firm silken tofu or
    vegan cream cheese
½ cup natural sugar
¼ cup plain unsweetened almond milk or
    other nondairy milk, or more if needed
1 teaspoon freshly squeezed lemon juice

1 teaspoon vanilla extract
6 vegan shortbread cookies,
    crumbled (about 1½ cups)
1½ to 2 cups fresh berries
    (raspberries, blueberries, or sliced
    strawberries, or a combination)
4 fresh mint sprigs

Drain the cashews. Place the cashews in a dry food processor or high-speed blender and process until finely ground. Loosen the cashews from the processor or blender. Add the tofu, sugar, almond milk, lemon juice, and vanilla. Process for several minutes, until completely smooth, scraping down the sides of the machine as needed. If the mixture is too thick, add a little more almond milk.

Transfer the cashew cream to a bowl. Add the cookies and all but 4 of the berries. Stir gently to combine. Divide the mixture equally among dessert glasses (wineglasses also work well here). Garnish with the reserved berries and mint sprigs.

butterscotch figgy bites

makes about 16 bites

This easy dessert is ideal for those times when you want a little something sweet. Considering they contain only three ingredients, these little bites are extremely rich tasting, with a great depth of flavor. Vegan butterscotch baking chips by Lieber's are readily available online. These are also good with semisweet vegan chocolate chips.

1½ cups dried but moist Calimyrna or
   Mission figs (just cut off the hard tips)
¾ cup semisweet vegan butterscotch
   (or chocolate) chips
1 cup bran cereal flakes

Preheat the oven to 350°F. Spray a mini muffin tin or an 8-inch square baking pan with nonstick cooking spray.

In a food processor, combine the figs, chips, and cereal flakes. Process until everything is well chopped and holds together when pressed.

Transfer the mixture to the prepared muffin tin, using about 1½ tablespoons per muffin cup, or spread in the baking pan, pressing evenly. Bake for 15 minutes in the muffin tin or 20 minutes in the baking pan. Let cool slightly before removing from the muffin pan and cutting into pieces.

baklava palmiers

makes 12 palmiers

Made with ready-made puff pastry (Pepperidge Farm brand is vegan), agave nectar, and your choice of ground pistachios or walnuts, these easy and elegant cookies are sure to satisfy when you crave the flavor of baklava but don't have time to make the traditional kind.

1 cup ground pistachios or walnuts
2 tablespoons natural sugar
Ground cinnamon

1 (10 by 14-inch) sheet vegan
   puff pastry, thawed
2 tablespoons agave nectar, plus
   more for drizzling (optional)

In a small bowl, combine the ground nuts, sugar, and as much cinnamon as you like in your baklava (from a pinch to ½ teaspoon). Mix to combine and set aside.

Roll out the puff pastry on a lightly floured work surface (you can roll it out between sheets of parchment paper if you like) into a 10 by 15-inch rectangle, trimming the edges if needed so you have straight sides.

Spread the nut mixture evenly on top of the pastry surface to cover, spreading it out to the edges, then drizzle with a thin drizzle of agave. Do not allow the agave to pool anywhere—it should be drizzled in a superthin stream.

Cut the pastry rectangle in half widthwise to create two long, narrow rectangles measuring 7½ by 10 inches each. Use your fingers to carefully roll one short end of one pastry rectangle toward the center, and then roll the opposite end toward the center so that

they meet in the center and look like two scrolls. Press gently to make sure the roll sticks together in the center. Repeat with the second strip of pastry, then wrap the pastry rolls separately in plastic wrap and refrigerate until firm, 1 to 2 hours.

Preheat the oven to 425°F. Line a baking sheet with parchment paper or a silicone baking mat. Use a sharp knife to slice one of the pastry rolls crosswise into 12 pieces and arrange them flat on the prepared baking sheet. (I only bake one roll at a time so they're baked fresh each time, but you can bake them both, if you prefer.)

Bake until the pastry is nicely browned, about 12 minutes. If they start to brown too much on the bottom after about 10 minutes, flip them for the last 2 minutes or longer, if needed. When the *palmiers* come out of the oven, you can drizzle them with more agave, if desired. Transfer the *palmiers* to a plate and serve warm.

raspberry zabaglione

serves 4

Traditionally made with egg yolks, sugar, and Marsala wine, zabaglione is typically served on its own or as a sauce over cake or fruit. This vegan version employs cashews and tofu to replace the eggs. It's great with fresh raspberries, but any kind of berries will do nicely.

¾ cup raw cashews, soaked in
   water for 3 hours or overnight
1 cup vegan cream cheese
   or firm silken tofu
½ cup natural sugar

½ cup unsweetened almond milk
   or other nondairy milk
½ cup dry Marsala
1 teaspoon vanilla extract
2 cups fresh raspberries

Drain the cashews. Place the cashews in a dry food processor or high-speed blender and process until finely ground. Loosen the cashews from the processor or blender. Add the cream cheese, sugar, almond milk, Marsala, and vanilla. Process for several minutes, until completely smooth, scraping down the sides of the machine as needed. If not using right away, transfer to a tightly covered container and refrigerate until serving time.

The zabaglione can be served chilled, at room temperature, or warm. If you prefer a warm zabaglione, transfer the mixture to a saucepan and heat over medium heat, stirring constantly, until warm. To serve, transfer to dessert glasses and top each serving with raspberries.

dessert chips and fresh fruit salsa

serves 6

Chips and salsa for dessert? Definitely—when your salsa is made with fresh fruit and your chips are sprinkled with cinnamon sugar! Mix and match the types of fruit used, depending on your personal preference and what's available. To make superfine sugar, process the sugar in a food processor or spice grinder until finely ground. This will help the sugar dissolve into the fruit.

1 mango, peeled, pitted, and chopped
1 cup chopped fresh pineapple
2 cups chopped fresh strawberries
1 or 2 kiwi fruits, peeled and chopped
1 Fuji or Gala apple, peeled,
   cored, and chopped
¼ cup dried sweetened cranberries
¼ cup toasted slivered almonds

2 teaspoons superfine natural sugar
   (see headnote) or agave nectar
6 (10-inch) flour tortillas
¼ cup vegan butter, melted
¼ to ⅓ cup natural sugar
2 teaspoons ground cinnamon
Fresh mint leaves, for garnish

In a large bowl, combine the mango, pineapple, strawberries, kiwis, apple, cranberries, almonds, and sugar. Toss gently to combine thoroughly. Cover and refrigerate for 15 minutes.

Preheat the oven to 350°F.

Place a tortilla on a work surface and brush one side of the tortilla with the melted butter. Combine the sugar and cinnamon in a small bowl and mix to combine. Sprinkle the tortilla with cinnamon sugar and cut it into wedges. Arrange the tortilla wedges on a large baking sheet in a single layer. Repeat with the remaining tortillas. (You may need to do this in batches.) Bake for 8 to 10 minutes. Cool the chips for about 10 minutes. Garnish the chilled salsa with the mint leaves and serve with the chips.

blueberry-chocolate trail mix bark

makes about 30 pieces

A new spin on old-fashioned almond bark, this version is the stuff dreams are made of—that is, if you dream about chocolate, nuts, pretzels, and blueberries! If dried blueberries are unavailable, or just for a variation, you can substitute dried cranberries, cherries, raisins, or other dried fruit in equal measure. This bark is also delicious made with vegan white chocolate.

12 ounces semisweet vegan
    chocolate chips
1½ cups chopped peanuts, pistachios,
    or almonds, or a combination

1½ cups thin salted pretzel
    sticks, coarsely chopped
1 cup chopped dried blueberries

Line a 9 by 13-inch baking dish with waxed paper. Melt the chocolate in a heatproof bowl over a saucepan of boiling water or in the microwave. Stir in the nuts, pretzels, and blueberries, then transfer the mixture to the baking dish. Spread the mixture evenly, smoothing out the top as much as possible. Refrigerate until firm, about 20 minutes. Invert the bark onto a cutting board and peel off the waxed paper. Cut the bark into pieces.

chocolate-roasted strawberries with almond butter cream

serves 4

This is a great way to use those large less-than-sweet strawberries we sometimes get during the off-season. In addition to being delicious over the almond butter cream, the roasted berries are great served alone or spooned over vegan ice cream or pound cake.

STRAWBERRIES
1 pint large fresh strawberries, hulled
¼ cup chopped or grated
   semisweet vegan chocolate
1 tablespoon natural sugar
1 tablespoon vegan butter,
   cut into small pieces

ALMOND BUTTER CREAM
1 cup vegan cream cheese or
   extra-firm silken tofu
⅓ cup almond butter
½ cup natural sugar
1 teaspoon vanilla extract

To roast the strawberries: Preheat the oven to 400°F. Arrange the strawberries, cut side down, in a single layer in a shallow 8-inch baking dish.

In a small bowl or food processor, combine the chocolate, sugar, and butter and pulse or mix to combine and make crumbly. Sprinkle the mixture over the berries and roast until the strawberries soften and the chocolate melts, about 8 minutes.

While the strawberries are roasting, make the almond butter cream: Combine the cream cheese, almond butter, sugar, and vanilla in a high-speed blender or food processor. Process until very smooth and well blended. Divide among 1-cup dessert dishes and refrigerate until needed.

Allow the strawberries to cool for a few minutes before serving. Spoon the strawberries over the almond butter cream and serve immediately.

peach melba crisp

serves 4

The classic dessert featuring peaches, raspberries, and vanilla ice cream was created in the late 1800s by Escoffier to honor opera singer Nellie Melba. Here two luscious fruits are combined in a crisp and served with vegan vanilla ice cream.

4 cups sliced fresh or frozen peaches
¼ to ½ cup natural sugar (depending
on the sweetness of your fruit)
2 cups fresh or frozen raspberries

2 cups vegan granola
¼ cup vegan butter, cut into small pieces
Vegan vanilla ice cream, for serving

Preheat the oven to 375°F. Lightly grease a shallow 1½-quart baking dish.

Place the peaches in the prepared baking dish. Sprinkle with the sugar and toss to combine, then spread the peaches evenly in the baking dish. Top with the raspberries.

Pulse the granola and butter in a food processor to break down the granola a bit and distribute the butter. Do not overprocess. Sprinkle the fruit with the granola mixture. Cover and bake for 15 minutes, then uncover and bake for 10 minutes longer to crisp the top. Let cool slightly, and serve with the ice cream.

"fruidités" with coconut-pineapple dip

serves 6 to 8

If you enjoy munching on the sliced raw vegetables known as crudités, then you're bound to love this dessert version I call "fruidités" that's made with sliced fresh fruit and a sweet, creamy dip.

8 ounces vegan cream cheese,
   at room temperature
½ cup unsweetened coconut milk
¼ cup shredded unsweetened coconut
2 mangos, peeled, pitted,
   and cut into chunks

2 apples, cored and cut into wedges
½ fresh pineapple, peeled,
   cored, and cut into sticks
2 cups fresh strawberries

In a food processor, combine the cream cheese, coconut milk, and 3 tablespoons of the shredded coconut and process until smooth and creamy. Transfer to a small bowl and sprinkle with the remaining 1 tablespoon coconut. Arrange in the center of a serving platter and surround the bowl with the cut fruit, arranged aesthetically. Serve at once. If not serving right away, keep the various elements separated, covered, and refrigerated until close to serving time. Bring to room temperature when ready to serve so that the flavors of the fruits are more vibrant.

(If you cut the apple wedges ahead of time, you should place them in a bowl of cold water with a couple of tablespoons of lemon juice added to keep the cut surface of the apples from turning brown. Drain and blot dry when ready to serve.)

avocado mousse with raspberries

serves 4

Creamy avocados are the star of this simple and delicious mousse that can be whipped up in just minutes. I love this creamy mousse topped with raspberries, but for extra raspberry goodness, you can also fold some halved or quartered raspberries into the mousse itself.

2 Hass avocados, pitted and peeled
2 tablespoons freshly squeezed lime juice
½ cup confectioners' sugar
⅓ cup almond milk or other nondairy milk
1 cup fresh raspberries

In a food processor, combine the avocados and lime juice and process until smooth. Add the confectioners' sugar and almond milk and process until creamy and well blended. Transfer to dessert dishes and serve immediately, or cover and refrigerate until chilled. To serve, top with the raspberries.

mango fried rice pudding

serves 4

This twist on rice pudding (and fried rice) is made with leftover cooked rice that you stir-fry with chopped mangos and a little sugar. You then stir in as much coconut milk as you like to make it firm or creamy to suit your own taste.

1 tablespoon vegan butter
¼ cup natural sugar
2 cups cold cooked basmati rice
2 mangos, peeled, pitted, and chopped

½ cup unsweetened coconut milk
2 tablespoons chopped pistachios (optional)

Melt the butter in a medium skillet over medium heat. Add the sugar and stir until melted. Add the rice and mangos and stir-fry until heated through. Stir in the coconut milk. To serve, spoon into dessert glasses and sprinkle with the pistachios, if using.

pumpkin brownies

makes 9 brownies

Chocolate and pumpkin pair well in these moist, cake-like brownies. You can add ½ cup chopped toasted pecans or walnuts, if you like.

1 cup canned solid-pack pumpkin
½ cup natural sugar
½ cup unsweetened cocoa powder
¼ cup pure maple syrup
1 teaspoon vanilla extract

1 teaspoon ground cinnamon
¼ teaspoon ground nutmeg
¼ teaspoon ground ginger or allspice
¾ cup unbleached all-purpose flour
1½ teaspoons baking powder

Preheat the oven to 350°F. Generously grease an 8-inch square baking pan.

In a food processor, combine the pumpkin, sugar, cocoa powder, maple syrup, vanilla, cinnamon, nutmeg, and ginger. Blend until smooth. Add the flour and baking powder and pulse to combine.

Scrape the batter evenly into the prepared pan. Bake for about 30 minutes or until a toothpick skewer inserted in the center comes out clean. Let cool before cutting into squares.

peanut butter and banana ice cream

serves 4

With only three ingredients, no dairy, no added sugar, and no ice-cream maker, this ice-cream treat seems almost too good to be true. But believe it. Serve alone or adorned with chocolate syrup and chopped nuts.

**3 to 4 very ripe bananas, peeled, cut
    into small chunks, and frozen**
½ cup peanut butter
2 tablespoons almond milk

Remove the frozen banana chunks from the freezer about 5 minutes before using and place them in a food processor. Pulse to break up the bananas, then add the peanut butter and almond milk and process until well mixed, scraping down the sides of the food processor as needed.

Scrape the mixture into a 1-quart plastic container with a tight-fitting lid. If you like soft-serve ice cream, it could be eaten immediately. If you prefer it a bit firmer, cover tightly and place in the freezer for 30 minutes to 1 hour, depending on how soft you like it. For an even firmer ice cream, keep it in the freezer for 3 to 4 hours. (If it freezes for longer than 4 hours, it will be quite hard, in which case it should be removed from the freezer about 10 minutes before serving so that it can temper and become slightly softened.) Properly stored, it will keep well in the freezer for up to 1 week.

my thai sundaes with green tea syrup

serves 4

These refreshing sundaes are the perfect ending to a spicy Thai dinner. Make the green tea syrup in advance so it has time to chill. You can also make the gingersnap topping in advance to save time when ready to serve.

½ cup brewed green tea
2 tablespoons natural sugar
½ cup crumbled gingersnaps
¼ cup flaked unsweetened coconut

1 teaspoon finely grated lime zest
1 pint vegan coconut ice cream
¼ cup crushed roasted unsalted peanuts

Combine the tea and sugar in a small saucepan over medium-high heat and bring to a boil. Lower the heat to a simmer and cook until the mixture becomes syrupy and is reduced by half. Remove from the heat and set aside to cool. If serving right away, transfer the syrup to a small bowl and place in the refrigerator or freezer to hasten the cooling process.

In a bowl, combine the gingersnap crumbs, coconut, and lime zest and stir to combine.

Place a small scoop of ice cream into the bottom of each dessert dish. Top each with about 2 tablespoons of the gingersnap mixture. Top with additional ice cream, then top with the remaining crumb mixture and the peanuts. Drizzle each with a small amount of the chilled green tea syrup and serve immediately.

chocolate chip–cherry ice cream

serves 4

With just a few ingredients and no ice-cream maker, you can whip up a delicious homemade vegan ice cream in minutes. Just be sure to keep cut-up bananas on hand in the freezer. The chocolate chips will remain fairly solid in the ice cream (which is fine), but if you prefer less texture, you'll need to soften the chocolate chips slightly before adding them to the food processor.

2 bananas, peeled, cut into small chunks, and frozen
½ cup semisweet vegan chocolate chips, at room temperature or slightly melted

2 tablespoons almond butter
1¼ cups pitted fresh cherries

Remove the frozen bananas from the freezer about 5 minutes before using. In a food processor, combine the bananas, chocolate chips, almond butter, and 1 cup of the cherries. Pulse to break up and then process until well mixed. Add the remaining ¼ cup cherries and pulse to combine, leaving some bits of cherry intact.

Scrape the mixture into a 1-quart plastic container with a tight-fitting lid. If you enjoy soft ice cream, you can eat it now. Otherwise, cover tightly and place in the freezer for 30 minutes to 1 hour, depending on how soft you like it. For an even firmer ice cream, keep it in the freezer for 3 to 4 hours. (If it freezes for longer than 4 hours, it will be quite hard, in which case it should be removed from the freezer about 10 minutes before serving so that it can temper and become slightly softened.) Properly stored, it will keep well in the freezer for up to 1 week.

metric conversions and equivalents

metric conversion formulas

to convert	multiply
Ounces to grams	Ounces by 28.35
Pounds to kilograms	Pounds by .454
Teaspoons to milliliters	Teaspoons by 4.93
Tablespoons to milliliters	Tablespoons by 14.79
Fluid ounces to milliliters	Fluid ounces by 29.57
Cups to milliliters	Cups by 236.59
Cups to liters	Cups by .236
Pints to liters	Pints by .473
Quarts to liters	Quarts by .946
Gallons to liters	Gallons by 3.785
Inches to centimeters	Inches by 2.54

approximate metric equivalents

weight

¼ ounce	7 grams
½ ounce	14 grams
¾ ounce	21 grams
1 ounce	28 grams
1¼ ounces	35 grams
1½ ounces	42.5 grams
1⅔ ounces	45 grams
2 ounces	57 grams
3 ounces	85 grams
4 ounces (¼ pound)	113 grams
5 ounces	142 grams
6 ounces	170 grams
7 ounces	198 grams
8 ounces (½ pound)	227 grams
16 ounces (1 pound)	454 grams
35.25 ounces (2.2 pounds)	1 kilogram

volume

¼ teaspoon	1 milliliter
½ teaspoon	2.5 milliliters
¾ teaspoon	4 milliliters
1 teaspoon	5 milliliters
1¼ teaspoons	6 milliliters
1½ teaspoons	7.5 milliliters
1¾ teaspoons	8.5 milliliters
2 teaspoons	10 milliliters
1 tablespoon (½ fluid ounce)	15 milliliters
2 tablespoons (1 fluid ounce)	30 milliliters
¼ cup	60 milliliters
⅓ cup	80 milliliters
½ cup (4 fluid ounces)	120 milliliters
⅔ cup	160 milliliters
¾ cup	180 milliliters
1 cup (8 fluid ounces)	240 milliliters
1¼ cups	300 milliliters
1½ cups (12 fluid ounces)	360 milliliters
1⅔ cups	400 milliliters
2 cups (1 pint)	460 milliliters
3 cups	700 milliliters
4 cups (1 quart)	0.95 liter
1 quart plus ¼ cup	1 liter
4 quarts (1 gallon)	3.8 liters

length

⅛ inch	3 millimeters
¼ inch	6 millimeters
½ inch	1¼ centimeters
1 inch	2½ centimeters
2 inches	5 centimeters
2½ inches	6 centimeters
4 inches	10 centimeters
5 inches	13 centimeters
6 inches	15¼ centimeters
12 inches (1 foot)	30 centimeters

oven temperatures

To convert Fahrenheit to Celsius, subtract 32 from Fahrenheit, multiply the result by 5, then divide by 9.

description	fahrenheit	celsius	british gas mark
Very cool	200°	95°	0
Very cool	225°	110°	¼
Very cool	250°	120°	½
Cool	275°	135°	1
Cool	300°	150°	2
Warm	325°	165°	3
Moderate	350°	175°	4
Moderately hot	375°	190°	5
Fairly hot	400°	200°	6
Hot	425°	220°	7
Very hot	450°	230°	8
Very hot	475°	245°	9

common ingredients and their approximate equivalents

1 cup uncooked white rice = 185 grams

1 cup all-purpose flour = 140 grams

1 stick butter (4 ounces • ½ cup • 8 tablespoons) = 110 grams

1 cup butter (8 ounces • 2 sticks • 16 tablespoons) = 220 grams

1 cup brown sugar, firmly packed = 225 grams

1 cup granulated sugar = 200 grams

Information compiled from a variety of sources, including *Recipes into Type* by Joan Whitman and Dolores Simon (Newton, MA: Biscuit Books, 2000); *The New Food Lover's Companion* by Sharon Tyler Herbst (Hauppauge, NY: Barron's, 1995); and *Rosemary Brown's Big Kitchen Instruction Book* (Kansas City, MO: Andrews McMeel, 1998).

index